Real Stories from the Rink

Real Stories from the Rink

BRIAN McFARLANE

ILLUSTRATIONS BY STEVE NEASE

Tundra Books

Text copyright © 2002 by Brian McFarlane
Illustrations copyright © 2002 by Steve Nease

Published in Canada by Tundra Books,
481 University Avenue, Toronto, Ontario M5G 2E9

Published in the United States by Tundra Books of Northern New York,
P.O. Box 1030, Plattsburgh, New York 12901

Library of Congress Control Number: 2002103702

National Library of Canada Cataloguing in Publication Data

McFarlane, Brian, 1931-
Real stories from the rink / Brian McFarlane ; illustrated by Steve Nease.

ISBN 0-88776-604-8

1. Hockey—History—Juvenile literature. I. Nease, Steve II. Title.

GV847.25.M345 2002   j796.962'09   C2002-901394-1

We acknowledge the support of the Canada Council for the Arts and the Ontario Arts Council
for our publishing program.

We acknowledge the financial support of the Government of Canada through the Book Publishing
Industry Development Program for our publishing activities.

Design: Blaine Herrmann

Printed and bound in Canada

1 2 3 4 5 6   07 06 05 04 03 02

To the proud members of the Canadian Men's and Women's Gold Medal-winning hockey teams at Salt Lake City, 2002 – champions all.
B. M.

To my wife and sons, with whom I have spent so many enjoyable hours at the rink.
S. N.

CONTENTS

CHAPTER 1

THE GOOD OLD HOCKEY GAME

The First Organized Game

Who invented hockey? On March 3, 1875, in Montreal, a group of McGill students, led by a man named James Creighton, played what was probably the first game of organized hockey. Others point out that a form of hockey, or "hurley" as it was often called, was played on frozen ponds and rivers in eastern Canada as early as 1800. But it was Creighton who organized the game and brought it indoors.

Because Creighton's game was played inside the old Victoria rink, a number of rules were adopted. Each team was limited to nine players, while in outdoor shinny any number could play. For the indoor game, the rubber ball usually used for a puck was discarded and a flat, circular piece of wood was used instead. (The word "puck" might have come from the old Gaelic word *puc* meaning a blow or hit – as in "He gave him a puck across the ankles.") Goals were devised – two poles or flags planted in the ice – and it's possible that hockey's first two goaltenders appeared in this game. The ice surface was the same size as most NHL rinks today, and there were team positions, a referee, and goal judges to control the play.

Others may argue, but James Creighton, who organized that game, deserves the title "Father of Hockey." And Montreal's claim to be the site of the first organized indoor hockey game has been backed by most hockey historians. One of them – Bill Fitsell of Kingston, Ontario – states, "That first game ended on a stunning note. 'Heads were bashed, benches smashed and the ladies who attended the game fled in fear and confusion.'"

How about These Rules?

In the early days of the game, hockey men were always arguing over the rules of the game. Should goal nets be allowed? How many men on a team? One referee or two? Should goalies be allowed to flop to the ice?

The following rule changes were proposed at the turn of the last century by the president of the Ottawa club, Mr. T. Emmett Quinn.

1. To increase scoring opportunities, the puck should be painted green and reduced to half its present size, thus making it more difficult for goaltenders to see and to stop.

2. Players should be compelled to carry enough bills in their pockets to pay any fines they may receive on the spot.

3. Instead of giving a player a minor penalty, the referee should stop the play, take the offender to the side boards and have an earnest discussion with him for a few minutes, so that he might reform him.

Mr. Quinn thought the proposed changes were good ones, but his colleagues disagreed and voted them down unanimously. Too bad. It would have been interesting to see if goalies could stop green pucks that were about the size of golf balls.

Getting Charlie to the Game

During the 1902 hockey season, a Montreal team left by train for Ottawa and a big game that night with the Ottawa Senators. But Charlie Liffiton, one of Montreal's star players, was not on board. Liffiton, like most of the other players, had a day job. His boss was not a hockey fan, and so he refused to let Liffiton off work early to join his teammates on the noon train for Ottawa.

Charlie's coach and the team manager pleaded with Liffiton's boss. "Charlie works nine to five like all my other employees," they were told. They knew their team's chances against Ottawa were slim if Liffiton was not in the Montreal lineup. So they chartered a special train for their star player.

When Liffiton was released from work that day, promptly at five o'clock p.m., he ran to the train station and hopped aboard the "special." With Charlie safely aboard as the only passenger, the train raced to Ottawa and arrived there just twenty minutes ahead of game time. The train's passenger leaped into a horse-drawn sleigh, which dashed off to the arena. There, Liffiton threw on his uniform and jumped on the ice, just in time for the opening face-off.

To have Liffiton in the Montreal lineup, team management paid $114 to the railroad company for the special train. But was it worth it? Liffiton, who was averaging a goal a game that season, was the best player on the ice, leading Montreal to a 4–2 victory.

Almost Everyone Got in Free

Montrealers have always had a passion for hockey and have always been rabid supporters of their home-town hockey teams. Their enthusiasm is responsible, at least in part, for the record number of Stanley Cups that have found their way to Montreal.

Shortly after the turn of the 20th century, there was great excitement in Montreal over a play-off game between the Montreal Wanderers and a team from Ottawa. On the street, in the hotels, and everywhere people congregated there was only one topic: who will win the big game? Tickets for the match sold for as high as twenty dollars apiece – about the same as what a new bicycle would cost, at a time when a school teacher might earn $300 a year – and they were snapped up within minutes. When evening came, hundreds of fans had already formed a long line, hoping for last-minute standing-room tickets.

The mob grew restless and advanced toward the arena. Thousands were soon battling for entrance into the rink. Some had tickets, but most did not. Ticket holders of choice seats were held up in the rush. They were pushed and prodded from behind and angry words flew. Hats were knocked off and stepped on, women fainted, clothes were torn, and rubber overshoes were lost in the scrimmage. Thirty Montreal policemen and eighty arena ushers tried in vain to stop the excited intruders. Some fans even scaled the walls of the arena, risking their lives climbing over the big electric-light sign, and smashed in windows on the upper level.

Pud Glass, who starred for Montreal, said he and the other Wanderers had no idea about the near-riot that had occurred while they were in their dressing room preparing to go on the ice. And who won the game? The Montreal Wanderers!

Creating a League with Two Dozen Players

It would be impossible to operate the National Hockey League without hiring hundreds of players for the thirty teams involved in the game. But at one time a professional league flourished in Canada made up of only twenty-four players – fewer players than each one of today's NHL teams employs. The league was the Pacific Coast Hockey Association, organized in 1911.

This little league was the brainchild of brothers Frank and Lester Patrick. The Patrick brothers were men of great vision. They added blue lines to the ice. They introduced assists to the game and numerals to the players' jerseys. Their Pacific Coast Hockey Association had three teams, all based in British Columbia: Vancouver, Victoria, and New Westminster. The Patrick brothers built new arenas in Vancouver and Victoria, and they had artificial ice installed, the first in Canada. They raided eastern Canada for talent and paid big money to the select handful of stars they signed. Each man was expected to play almost a full sixty minutes of every game during the fifteen-game schedule.

It didn't take the Patricks long to win the Stanley Cup. Frank Patrick was not only a founder of the league, but also one of its greatest stars. In 1917, serving as playing manager, he helped his Vancouver Millionaires sweep the Ottawa Senators in a Stanley Cup play-off series. In one game, playing defense, he rushed repeatedly up the ice and scored six goals.

In 1926, when hockey in western Canada collapsed, the Patricks sold all their players to NHL clubs, then joined two of those clubs as managers. Craig Patrick, Lester's grandson, carries on the famous family name as general manager of the Pittsburgh Penguins.

Hockey Night in . . . the U.S.A.

Would you be surprised to learn that the first televised hockey game in North America wasn't seen in Canada? And that it took place more than sixty years ago? During the 1940–41 NHL season, a hockey game between the New York Rangers and the Montreal Canadiens at Madison Square Garden stands out as a history-making event. For the very first time, hockey fans in the New York area could follow the on-ice action in their living rooms – thanks to a miraculous new invention called television.

Only a few hundred fans watched the first hockey telecast because there were only about 300 TV sets in all of New York City. Each television that was tuned in to the game showed a grainy picture on a tiny screen of about 7 inches, less than 18 centimeters. Fans complained about how hard it was to follow the puck on their screens.

It wasn't until a dozen years later, during the 1952–53 season, that the first hockey games were televised in Canada. Instead of the one camera used in that first televised game in the U.S., four or five cameras were needed. Today, it is possible to have as many as fourteen cameras covering an important game – in the arena, in the intermission studio, in the goal nets, over the ice – including as many as six replay cameras.

Dick Rondeau's Best Game

Most high scorers, when you ask them to name their most memorable game, find it hard to choose just one. Not former U.S. college star Dick Rondeau, who was a top scorer for the Dartmouth College Indians many years ago. Dartmouth dominated college hockey during World War II, and in 1944 the Indians achieved their most one-sided victory, a 30–0 whitewashing of Middlebury College in Vermont. Rondeau was a dazzling, unstoppable scorer in this game, combining 12 goals with 11 assists for 23 points – a once-in-a-lifetime performance.

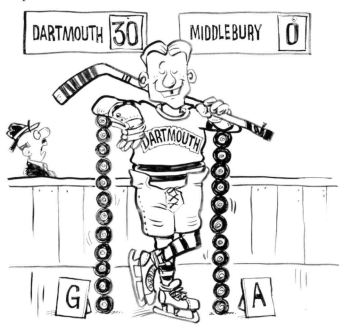

Incidentally, from 1942 to 1946, Dartmouth won thirty consecutive games, a U.S. college record. And in 1992 – 93, Paul Kariya led the Maine Black bears to a 42-1-2 record, the best in U.S. college history.

The Coach Pulled his Goalie – With Astonishing Results

In the late 1950s, the St. Catharines Tee Pees faced off against the powerful Toronto Marlboros in an important Junior A play-off game. By the last minute of play, the Marlies were leading 5–4. Not wanting to get caught in the rush to the parking lot, many fans headed for the exits of the St. Catharines Arena.

With 28 seconds left on the clock, there was a face-off in the St. Catharines zone. That's when Tee Pees' coach Rudy Pilous decided to take the biggest gamble of his career. He pulled his goaltender and sent out an extra attacker. The fans thought Pilous had lost his mind. No coach had ever left his net empty with the face-off only a few feet away. The Marlboros couldn't wait for the puck to be dropped. That empty net looked so inviting! Meanwhile, the home-town fans howled their displeasure. They booed the man who seemed to be handing the game to their opponents on a silver platter.

When the puck was dropped, the Marlies banged away at it, all of them eager to fire the disk into the empty net. But somehow it was a Tee Pee, Hugh Barlow, who came up with the rubber. Barlow found an opening and raced down the ice. With just 12 seconds to play he banged in the tying goal.

There was pandemonium in the arena. In the parking lot, fans leaped out of their cars and raced back to reclaim their seats for the overtime.

Pilous didn't have to take any more big risks that night. His Tee Pees won the game and went on to capture the Memorial Cup that season.

The Flyers' Fabulous Streak

How long can a team go without losing? Long undefeated streaks are rare in sports today. But occasionally they happen and when they do, fans, coaches, and players alike wonder how long they will last. In all of pro sports, the longest undefeated streak belongs to the 1979–80 Philadelphia Flyers. It was a streak that began in October and lasted through December. After losing the second game of the season to Atlanta, the Flyers topped Toronto 4–3, and that was the beginning of a remarkable romp around the NHL.

Flyers coach Pat Quinn deserves most of the credit for the streak. He had his players emphasize speed and quick passes, and he eliminated much of the brawling that had been a longtime Flyers trademark.

When the streak reached twenty-eight games, the Flyers tied the NHL record held by the Montreal Canadiens. Two nights later they set a new mark of twenty-nine with a win over Boston. In December they snapped the pro sports record of thirty-three games established by basketball's Los Angeles Lakers.

But all good things must end, including undefeated streaks. The end came for the Flyers in game number thirty-six, when they were walloped 7–1 by Minnesota, sealing their record of twenty-five wins and ten ties.

CHAPTER 2
POOR PLAY

Let's Try to Score at Least One Goal

Can you imagine any team in the NHL going eight straight games without scoring a single goal? Not even a flukey one? Let's look back on a pioneer edition of the Chicago Blackhawks and see how pathetic they were.

During the 1928–29 season, the Blackhawks set records for hopelessness that have lasted for more than seventy years. It was their third NHL season, and the Blackhawks won a mere seven games in a schedule of forty-four. During one stretch they were shutout eight straight times. And there were more shutouts to come. Over the course of the season, the Hawks were blanked twenty-one times, almost 50 percent of the time. Opposing goalies couldn't wait to face them.

All their so-called scorers were pitiful, managing only thirty-three goals all season, less than one per game. Forward Vic Ripley led the Hawk scorers with 11 goals and 2 assists for 13 points – Darryl Sittler of the Maple Leafs almost equaled Ripley's season production in one game in 1976, when he scored a record ten points against Boston.

Fortunately, in 1928–29, the Hawks had Charlie "Chuck" Gardiner in goal, or they might not have won a single game. Gardiner was among the league's best netminders, posting five shutouts and a 1.93 goals-against average in forty-four games. Gardiner was a good-natured fellow who never blamed his teammates for their shortcomings. Otherwise, he might have asked, "Can't anyone here play this game?"

The Team That Won the Fewest Games

When the NHL was formed in November 1917, there were five charter members of the league. Then, before the first puck was dropped, one of the five teams, the Quebec Bulldogs, decided to wait another season before joining the new circuit. That left four teams – the Montreal Canadiens, the Montreal Wanderers, the Ottawa Senators, and the Toronto Arenas. Soon there was to be only three.

The Montreal Wanderers not only hold the record for the shortest stay in the NHL, they recorded the fewest wins. The Wanderers' proudest moment came on December 19, 1917, when they edged Toronto 10–9 in their home opener in front of 700 fans. It was their one and only victory in the NHL.

Two weeks later, on January 2, 1918, their home arena burned to the ground. Homeless, the team ceased operations and never returned.

Hockey Riot in Montreal

March 17, 1955, will be long remembered for an ugly riot that took place inside and outside the Montreal Forum. NHL President Clarence Campbell had decided to suspend Maurice "Rocket" Richard, the greatest star of the Montreal Canadiens, for his attack on a Boston player and for striking a game official during a previous game at the Boston Garden. The harsh suspension would keep Richard out of the remaining games in the regular season and all play-off games that spring.

The fans who filled the Forum on the night of St. Patrick's Day were in an ugly mood before the opening face-off against Detroit. Their anger and frustration deepened when the Red Wings slapped in four fast goals in the opening few minutes. The Canadiens could see the league championship slipping away. Richard, standing in the Forum corridor, was aware that his chance to win his first individual scoring crown was in jeopardy as well.

Midway through the first period Clarence Campbell slipped into the Forum and took his seat among the fans. They hurled slurs at the man who had suspended their hero. A hoodlum punched the league president, and another fan squeezed a ripe tomato over Campbell's head. Police rushed to the scene, and while they were escorting Campbell to the safety of a dressing room, a tear-gas bomb exploded on the ice. The fire marshall ordered the building evacuated and people fled in near panic toward the exits. The game was canceled and forfeited to Detroit.

Outside the Forum fans went on a wild rampage. They threw rocks and bottles through the windows of the arena. Then a howling mob surged down St. Catherine Street, smashing windows, looting shops, and setting fires.

The forfeited game let the Red Wings capture the league title for the seventh consecutive season and the Stanley Cup that year. The suspension cost Rocket Richard any chance he had of winning his first scoring crown. Teammate Boom Boom Geoffrion edged him out by a single point, 75 to 74, only to be booed by his own fans for beating the Rocket.

Holt Holds Penalty Records

On March 11, 1979, at the Philadelphia Spectrum, Randy Holt of the Los Angeles Kings declared a one-man war against the Flyers' Frank Bathe. Holt racked up nine penalties totaling 67 minutes – an NHL record. He collected one minor penalty, three majors, two ten-minute misconducts, and three game misconducts, all in the first period. Bathe, the Flyer who scrapped with Holt several times in the opening frame, finished the game with 55 penalty minutes, the second highest single-game total ever.

While Holt still holds the single-game record for penalty minutes, he failed to hold on to the nine-penalty record he set that night. On March 31, 1991, Chris Nilan, then with the Boston Bruins, took ten penalties in a game against Hartford.

Murder on Ice

There have been many serious injuries in NHL hockey games but only one fatality: in 1968, Minnesota's Bill Masterton died accidentally after colliding with a rival player and then striking his head on the ice. But the death of star player Owen McCourt in the old Federal League in 1907 was said to be the result of a deliberate assault. McCourt's team-mates called it "murder on ice," and there were demands that the player who delivered the fatal blow be jailed for the rest of his life.

McCourt was the scoring star of the team from Cornwall, Ontario. On March 6, 1907, playing against a tough Ottawa squad, McCourt became involved in a fight with Art Throop. Soon all the players on the ice were involved in the pushing and shoving, including an Ottawa player named Charlie Masson. Witnesses said Masson attacked McCourt, smashing him over the head with his hockey stick. McCourt was rushed to the nearest hospital, and within hours he died.

Masson was arrested and charged with the murder of Owen McCourt. He faced a lifetime prison term. But at his trial, witnesses gave conflicting testimony. Some testified under oath they saw Masson wield the stick that caused McCourt's death. Others said McCourt had been struck on the head by another Ottawa player. Finally the judge said he could not determine which player had delivered the fatal blow. Charlie Masson was acquitted of all charges and set free.

The Ottawa team, distressed over the death of a rival player, decided to bow out of hockey and canceled all their remaining games, even though the league championship was within their reach.

The Longest Suspensions

Back in 1927, during a play-off game between the Boston Bruins and the Ottawa Senators, Bill Coutu, a rugged veteran with the Bruins, lost his temper following referee Jerry Laflamme's call. He turned and assaulted Laflamme and knocked him flat. Then Coutu, still boiling, turned on linesman Bill Bell and tackled him to the ice. Coutu's outrageous behavior took place right in front of NHL president Frank Calder, who sentenced Coutu to a lifetime suspension and fined him $100. Five years later, the suspension was lifted – but it was too late for Coutu to resume his career.

On March 9, 1947, NHL president Clarence Campbell sentenced Billy Taylor of the Rangers and Don Gallinger of the Bruins to lifetime suspensions after he discovered they were associating with gamblers (although Campbell stressed that no fix of any hockey game was involved or even attempted). These two suspensions were not lifted until 1970, when both players were well into middle-age. Taylor returned to hockey as a scout; Gallinger never returned to the game.

Two of the longest suspensions to NHL players for their actions on the ice occurred during the year 2000. On February 23, Boston's Marty McSorley smashed Donald Brashear of the Vancouver Canucks across the head with his stick and was suspended for twenty-three games. The sentence was later extended to one year. On November 11, Brad May of the Phoenix Coyotes swung his stick, slashing Columbus Blue Jackets forward Steve Heinze in the face. May was suspended for twenty games.

Rough body contact is part of hockey but extreme acts of violence should not be tolerated. If players knew they faced suspension for a full season – or for life – for deliberately slugging another player with their sticks, they might not be so quick to use them as weapons.

NHL Hockey Dies in Hamilton

For the 1924–25 NHL season, the league added six games to the schedule, and the extra workload – with no extra pay – caused grumbling around the league. Especially in Hamilton, Ontario.

The Hamilton Tigers had risen from last place to first, and the Stanley Cup was only a couple of play-off victories away. But before competing for the Stanley Cup, the Tigers wanted some compensation for the six extra games they had been forced to play. They figured $200 per player was fair.

"Forget compensation. There'll be no extra pay," roared the team owner. And Frank Calder, the league president, backed him up.

"Then we're going on strike," replied the players defiantly.

The league president immediately suspended the Tigers and named two other NHL clubs – Montreal and Toronto – to compete in the 1925 play-offs.

The player revolt cost Hamilton a splendid chance to win the Cup. And then, in the off-season, the Hamilton franchise was moved to New York where it was trans-formed into the New York Americans. And Hamilton has never again been home to an NHL team.

Bad Boys

Sometimes in the NHL, players lose their tempers and penalties result. The following records for bad behavior prove that a harsh body-contact game like hockey can give penalty timekeepers splitting headaches.

When Edmonton played Los Angeles on February 28, 1990, a total of eighty-five penalties were called. That's a record number for two teams in one game. The Oilers were penalized forty-four times, establishing a record for most penalties for one team in a game.

In one period of hockey how much trouble can two NHL clubs get into? On February 26, 1981, the Minnesota North Stars and the Boston Bruins combined for 67 penalties in the first period of the game. Minnesota earned 34 of the penalties to establish another NHL mark for bad behavior.

Can you name hockey's most penalized player? The career record-holder is Dave "Tiger" Williams who played with five NHL clubs over fourteen seasons. Williams sat out 3966 minutes in penalties – that's 66 hours and 10 minutes. One night in the Toronto penalty box, Williams was told to "sit down and be quiet" by penalty timekeeper Joe Lamantia. Williams gave Lamantia a wounded look and said, "Joe, if you're going to speak to me like that, I'm never coming back in here again."

Pay Up, Randall!

In February 1918, temperamental hockey player Ken Randall of Toronto argued with officials in an NHL game and was fined fifteen dollars. He was told that if the fifteen dollars, and other fines he owed in the amount of thirty-two dollars, were paid promptly, he would be allowed to play in Toronto's next game. If not, he would be suspended.

Prior to the game, Randall showed up with his pockets full of money and paid his fine. But a lot of the cash was in pennies – he spilled out more than 300 of them – and officials refused to accept the coins.

"But I'm paying in legal tender," Randall protested while his teammates smirked. When his protest was ignored, Randall placed the pennies in a neat stack atop the boards. That's when a Toronto player skating by impishly whacked the pile of pennies with his stick, scattering them all over the ice. Randall was forced to drop to his knees and gather up the pennies. He risked a delay-of-game penalty if he didn't get things cleaned up before the opening face-off. Then Randall exchanged the pennies for suitable folding money to make up his fine.

Dino Lands in Jail

It began as a minor altercation and then turned vicious. In a game at Maple Leaf Gardens during the 1987–88 season, winger Dino Ciccarelli of the Minnesota North Stars and Toronto defenseman Luke Richardson collided near the boards. Ciccarelli whacked Richardson over the head with his stick. He followed up with a solid punch to the mouth.

Similar incidents on the ice had happened numerous times in the NHL. Perhaps that's why Ciccarelli was so surprised when he was charged with assault and taken into custody. At his trial, Dino was told by the judge that the court took a dim view of violence on the ice. The hockey star (he scored 608 goals in the NHL over nineteen seasons) was convicted and handed a twenty-four-hour jail sentence plus a $1000 fine.

Released after a couple of hours in a cell, Ciccarelli called the verdict "ridiculous." As the first NHLer to receive a jail sentence for his on-ice behavior, Ciccarelli said, "Oh, it wasn't so bad behind bars. I met a big cop who was chewing a doughnut. Then I signed a few autographs for the other inmates and left."

Espo's Wild Ride

In the spring of 1973, the Boston Bruins were eliminated from the Stanley Cup play-offs by their archrivals, the New York Rangers. During the series, Bruins star Phil Esposito was hospitalized in Boston with a leg injury. The Bruins were holding their annual post-season party and they decided that Esposito must attend, bad leg and all. After some discussion they decided to kidnap him – for just a few hours.

While a few of the Bruins distracted the nurses on duty, other players wheeled Esposito – still in his hospital bed – down an elevator and out a side exit. Somehow a metal railing was broken during the escape. The Bruins guided the hospital bed and its famous patient down the avenue while drivers beeped their horns and moved out of the way. Led by Wayne Cashman and Bobby Orr, the players wheeled their leader around a corner with Orr shouting, "Left turn, Phil, signal a left." Espo's left arm could be seen waving from under the sheets.

When the Bruins were partied out, it was time to get Esposito back to the hospital. They wheeled him back, and were confronted by hospital officials who were not amused by the prank. They had been busy estimating the costs involved in fixing the broken railing. One of them presented the Bruins with a invoice calling for payment of several hundred dollars for "damages to hospital property."

Cashman and Orr quickly dealt with that dilemma. While Espo slept, his teammates slipped the invoice into the pocket of his pajamas.

Fotiu Famous for Practical Jokes

Former NHLer Nick Fotiu proudly claims the title "Hockey's Most Famous Practical Joker." During his long career, Fotiu tormented hundreds of teammates with his impish actions.

He recalls one of his best tricks: "I was with Calgary, and before practice one day I took all the towels stacked up in the dressing room and secretly smeared gobs of Vaseline in between the folds. It had worked like a charm before, especially when Lanny McDonald got the Vaseline smeared into his huge mustache. It was hilarious. But this time, after the guys had showered and used their towels, there was no reaction.

I took Bearcat Murray, our trainer, aside and said, 'Bearcat, those towels I filled with Vaseline – what happened to them?'

"He said, 'Geez, Nick, I didn't know you did that. I took those towels over to the visitors' dressing room. They were for the Canucks.'

"Can you imagine the Canucks drying off with those sticky towels?!

"There were a few sneaky things I did when I was with the Rangers," Fotiu continues, "Like putting talcum powder in the hair dryers and covering the earpiece of the telephone with black shoe polish. One day I took Phil Esposito's brand new white golf shoes and painted them bright orange. I learned that Phil hated creepy-crawlies, so I would collect cockroaches and slip them in his hockey bag. That drove him up the wall. There was the time I caught Mark Osborne about to spray shaving cream on my head – he thought I was asleep. I told him I owed him one and it was going to be memorable.

"A few days later I went down to the docks and bought some fish. I cut the fish into little pieces and stuck the pieces in Mark's uniform, tucking them into places where he wouldn't notice them. It wasn't long before that uniform really began to reek. Guys wouldn't even sit next to him on the bench. Other players would skate by him holding their sticks out like fishing rods. Geez, did he stink! That was one of my best efforts."

CHAPTER 3
BEHIND THE BENCH

Game on! But Where's the Coach?

During the 1988 Stanley Cup play-offs, in a game between the St. Louis Blues and the Chicago Blackhawks, Chicago coach Bob Murdoch called for a strategy meeting during the first intermission. He and his assistant coaches entered a small room next to the team dressing room. Murdoch, the last man in, slammed the door hard behind him. Maybe it was bit too hard, for when the meeting broke up, none of the coaches could get the door open again. Arena workers arrived on the scene, but they too were unable to open the door. Meanwhile, the fans grew restless and shouted at the helpless referee, "Let's play hockey!"

Suddenly, an arena worker saved the day. Riding up on a forklift truck, he wheeled his machine toward the door, crashed into it, and sent panels flying. The three coaches stumbled over the broken pieces, dusted themselves off, and returned sheepishly to their duties behind the Blackhawks bench.

A Surprise Gift for the Prime Minister

In 1972, Team Canada defeated the Soviets by the slimmest of margins in the memorable "series of the century" – and all Canadians rejoiced. Before leaving Moscow, Team Canada assistant coach John Ferguson began collecting autographs. On a hockey stick he had signatures of players from both teams. The stick was a memento Ferguson planned to treasure forever.

When Team Canada's flight touched down in Montreal, a huge reception awaited them. The players and coaches passed through a reception line where they were greeted by the Prime Minister of Canada at that time, Pierre Elliott Trudeau.

Ferguson, clutching his souvenir stick, made his way down the line behind his close friend, Canadiens defenseman Serge Savard. Savard and the Prime Minister shook hands. Then, to Fergie's amazement, he heard Savard say, "Mr. Prime Minister, my friend John Ferguson has brought you a special souvenir, all the way from Moscow. It's a hockey stick autographed by all the players."

"Thank you, John," said Mr. Trudeau, handing the stick to an aide. "What a wonderful gift."

What could Fergie do? He turned away, fretting and fuming while Savard chuckled over his pal's discomfort. At the same time, Savard kept his distance. He feared his friend might try to throttle him – right on national TV.

Coach and Referee in Slugfest

Can you imagine? At rinkside a coach in the NHL grabs a referee by the shirt and begins to pummel him. And the referee, just a little guy, begins punching back. Such a battle broke out on the night of March 14, 1933, at the Boston Garden.

It took place during overtime of a game between the Bruins and the Chicago Blackhawks. Boston had just pulled ahead 3–2 after three minutes of overtime, which in those days was not sudden-death but required a full ten minutes of extra play. When Boston forward Marty Barry scored from a scramble, Chicago manager/coach Tommy Gorman was furious. "The puck did not cross the goal line," he screamed at Bill Stewart, the referee. When referee Stewart (grandfather of current NHL referee Paul Stewart) skated close to the Chicago bench, Gorman reached out and grabbed him by the jersey. The coach began throwing punches at the startled official. The crowd roared when Stewart, a much smaller man, began punching right back.

Finally, Stewart broke free of Gorman's flailing fists. "You're outta the game, Gorman," he snarled, pointing a finger in the direction of the Chicago dressing room. When Gorman refused to budge, several policemen moved in and ejected him bodily. One by one, the Chicago players left the ice and followed Gorman to the dressing room. Some of them who hassled the police were threatened with a night in jail if they didn't behave.

Referee Stewart skated to center ice and pulled out his watch. He gave the Hawks exactly one minute to get some players back on the ice. When Gorman and the Hawks thumbed their noses at his ultimatum, he made his decision: the game was forfeited to the Bruins.

Stewart's handling of the situation must have impressed Chicago Blackhawks owner Major Fred McLaughlin. Four years later, McLaughlin persuaded Stewart to turn in his skates and coach his hockey team. Incredibly, the former referee and major-league baseball umpire guided the Hawks to the Stanley Cup in his first year behind the bench. A few months later, McLaughlin fired him.

Eddie Shore's Weird Behavior

Many years ago, Don Cherry, Canada's colorful hockey commentator, played four seasons on defense for Springfield, Massachusetts, of the American Hockey League. This gave him plenty of time to observe the oddball behavior of owner/manager/coach Eddie Shore, one of the most bizarre characters in hockey.

Springfield players were instructed by Shore never to tip a cab driver more than fifteen cents. As a result, cabbies tried to avoid picking up hockey players.

At contract time, Shore would grant a player bonus money for scoring 30 goals. But when the player reached 29 goals, he was likely to find himself riding the bench for the rest of the season.

If one of his goalies flopped to the ice too often in workouts, Shore would get a rope and tie him to the crossbar.

Shore needed goaltending help one season and traded for a player named Smith. When Smith arrived, Shore asked, "Where are your goal pads?" Smith answered, "Mr. Shore, I'm not a goalie, I'm a left winger."

One player traded to Springfield arrived in time to see the team working out in a hotel lobby. They were practicing dance routines.

Springfield's Black Aces were players who were in Shore's doghouse. Somehow they had fouled up and enraged him. They practiced but seldom played. Because they weren't playing hockey, they were required to paint the arena seats, sell programs at games, make popcorn, and blow up balloons for special events.

Referees and linesmen dreaded working games in Springfield. If a referee infuriated Shore, he might find himself locked in the officials' dressing room until Shore cooled off, or he might be locked out of the room – Shore kept the key to the door. If Shore felt the official was totally incompetent, he might denounce him over the public-address system in the arena.

Cherry laughs when he recalls one of his favorite stories about Shore. "Eddie was giving us a long list of instructions at practice one day. It was kinda boring so I glanced up at the clock, wondering how long he was gonna go on. He caught me not payin' attention, so he forced me to skate laps around the rink for the next four-and-a-half hours. He turned out the lights and left me there – skating in the dark."

When Mount Orval Erupted

In 1982–83, the Chicago Blackhawks were impressed with their rookie coach, Orval Tessier. Tessier had guided the Hawks from 30 wins and 72 points to 47 wins and 104 points – and a first place finish in the Norris Division – in his first season behind the bench. It was a stunning improvement, and Hawks fans believed they would soon be parading through the city with the Stanley Cup. Tessier, at season's end, would be named Coach-of-the-Year. He was the best thing to happen to Chicago since Bobby Hull. But Tessier's career took a sudden downturn in the play-offs, all because of a conversation with the media that lasted only a few seconds.

The Blackhawks, after losing only two of nine play-off games in eliminating the St. Louis Blues and the Minnesota North Stars, met one of the greatest teams ever assembled – the Edmonton Oilers – in the Conference finals. The Oilers bounced Chicago from the Stanley Cup chase in four straight games. During the series, Tessier exploded in anger and frustration. Livid with rage after suffering through 8–4 and 8–2 losses, Tessier told the media, "my players need eighteen heart transplants."

Those few ill-chosen words would cost Tessier all the respect he had earned in the dressing room and with the media. In time, it would cost him his job. Reporters began calling him Mount Orval, Lava Lips, and The Glowering Inferno. Veteran Hawks star Al Secord, stung by Tessier's remarks, engaged in a shouting match with his coach in the Hawks dressing room with the entire team backing him.

Tessier's loss of his players' respect soon coincided with a loss in the standings. The Hawks plunged from 104 points to 68 points in a season and a half. Manager Bob Pulford had seen and heard enough. Mount Orval was fired and never got a second chance to coach in the NHL.

Scotty Bowman and the Hungry Hockey Player

All NHL coaches love hungry hockey players – players who hunger for a goal, a victory, a Stanley Cup. But one of coach Scotty Bowman's players carried the idea of being hungry a bit too far one night.

George Morrison played for Bowman on the St. Louis Blues, but was not one of Bowman's favorite players. So, for most of the 1970–71 season, Morrison was used sparingly.

One night in Los Angeles, Morrison sat patiently on the bench through one period and then another. Thinking there was no way he was going to play that night, he convinced an usher to bring him a hot dog and a soft drink. Morrison started in on his snack, making sure Scotty Bowman was looking in the other direction.

Suddenly there was a penalty and Bowman shouted down the bench, "Morrison, get out there and kill off that penalty."

Morrison was stunned. He couldn't be caught eating in the middle of a game! He flipped the soft drink onto the floor. But what to do with the hot dog? Almost without thinking, he stuffed the hot dog down the cuff of his hockey glove and leaped over the boards.

In front of the Blues goal, the action was fierce. A rival player slammed into Morrison's elbow and knocked the hot dog loose. It flew high in the air with mustard and relish flying in all directions. When it landed, the goalie trapped it with his stick and scooped it into his net.

"I never did find out if Scotty knew it was me who had the hot dog in my glove," Morrison said, recalling the incident with obvious glee. "But I'm sure he suspected it was me. He must have, because it was a long time before he played me again."

During his brilliant career, Bowman wanted only the most dedicated players on his teams. Maybe that's why Morrison lasted only two seasons in St. Louis. Bowman went on to become the winningest coach in NHL history. During the 2000–01 season, he won his 2000th NHL game, making his win total the highest in NHL history. And on his retirement the next year, he had won a record nine Stanley Cups with three different teams – Montreal, Pittsburgh, and Detroit. He even named one of his sons Stanley, after the Stanley Cup. Hockey's greatest coach was inducted into the Hockey Hall of Fame in 1991.

When Coaches Lose Their Cool

NHL coaches often find it difficult to control their emotions during the course of an NHL season and during the play-offs. When they lose their cool, the results are unpredictable.

Roger Neilson, when he coached the Buffalo Sabres, threw sticks and a water bottle on the ice because he didn't care for the officiating in a game. Mike Milbury did the same thing when he coached a minor league club. Milbury also left the bench one night to run up to the organ loft, to admonish the organist for playing a number he thought was disrespectful to one of his players.

Tom Webster, coach of the L.A. Kings, hurled a hockey stick, javelin style, at a referee during an NHL game, hitting the official on the foot.

Billy Reay, when he coached Buffalo in the American Hockey League, got into a fistfight with the team's announcer. Murph Chamberlain, another Buffalo coach, threw a bucket of pucks on the ice while a game was in progress.

Jacques Demers and Mike Keenan are two NHL coaches who have been accused of tossing pennies on the ice to create a time-out during games.

Toe Blake of the Montreal Canadiens once stormed across the ice and punched a referee. He was fined $2000.

A coach of a junior team in western Canada once stripped to the waist during a game. Talk about getting hot under the collar!

Toronto's Punch Imlach once put on his skates at the Maple Leafs bench, opened the gate, and was about to skate out and argue a point with the referee, when he had second thoughts and retreated. Emile Francis of the New York Rangers once scooted around the rink to tell off a goal judge. Fans intervened and Francis found himself in the middle of a battle. His players had to climb over the high glass, leap into the throng, and rescue him.

Jack Adams of Detroit, with his team leading Toronto three games to one, jumped on the ice at the end of game four of the 1941 Stanley Cup finals and started punching referee Harwood. It marked a turning point in the series. Adams was suspended indefinitely and his team sagged – Toronto won three in a row and captured the Stanley Cup in what has been called hockey's greatest comeback.

CHAPTER 4

UNEXPECTED STARS

Twenty-four Years with the Same Team

Hall of Famer Alex Delvecchio played in more than 1500 NHL games, scored 456 goals and added 825 assists – all with the Detroit Red Wings. Delvecchio spent most of his twenty-four-year career performing in the huge shadow cast by teammate Gordie Howe.

"That never bothered me," Delvecchio says. "Gordie was the greatest player of all time. When you played with him, you just knew that good things were going to happen."

Delvecchio's career scoring stats would have been even more impressive if he hadn't encountered a prolonged slump during the 1969–70 season. Incredibly, he skated through the first thirty-two games of the season without scoring a goal. His many fans sent him dozens of good-luck charms to help him snap the jinx. Finally, Miss America came to his aid. Pamela Anne Eldred, of Birmingham, Michigan, had worn a small jeweled pin on her brassiere when she captured the Miss America title. She sent the pin to Delvecchio and wished him luck. He attached the pin to his hockey suspenders. Eureka! On New Year's Eve, 1969, he scored his first goal of the season in a 5–1 rout of Boston. Three nights later, with the pin firmly in place, he scored a hat trick against Philadelphia.

In the mid-seventies, Delvecchio became coach and general manager of the struggling Red Wings. He quickly turned the team around, silencing the critics who said he was too nice a person to be a coach.

Most Gentlemanly Player – Ever!

It's a fact. The tough guys in hockey get far more attention and publicity than the players who mind their own business and play by the rules. Why does the *NHL Official Guide & Record Book* list the players who take the most penalties (Tiger Williams, Dale Hunter, Marty McSorley, and others) and completely ignore those who take the fewest?

If the NHL Guide listed hockey's cleanest players, Val Fonteyne, a former Red Wing, might well be at the top of the list. During one stretch in his thirteen-year NHL career, Fonteyne played in 185 consecutive games without spending any time in the penalty box. His teammates kidded him:

"Val, if you ever do get another penalty, will you remember where to go?"

"Val, go take a look in the box. See what it's like in there."

Later in his career, Fonteyne managed to compile a second streak of 157 penalty-free games. A skinny player who excelled as a penalty killer, he spent only twenty-eight minutes in the box over the course of 820 NHL games. Fonteyne is the only player to complete three consecutive seasons without taking a single minor penalty, and the only one to compile five penalty-free seasons. Because he never fought, he never served a major penalty.

Fans who like to see records broken may have to wait for decades – perhaps forever – before someone comes along to break fewer hockey rules than hockey's perfect gentleman, Val Fonteyne.

First Woman in the Pro Game

Manon Rheaume retired from goaltending after breaking many of hockey's barriers. At age thirty, the Montreal native now plays forward when she plays at all. Recently she joined a sports manufacturing company in California – Mission Betty – which has developed a new skate designed specifically for women players.

Rheaume has had a unique career in both men's and women's hockey. At age eleven, she became the first female to play in the famed Quebec Pee Wee Tournament. At age nineteen, she became the first female to play goal for a team in the Quebec Junior league. In the early 1990s, Tampa Bay manager Phil Esposito signed her to a contract, and she made history by playing one period of a pre-season game against St. Louis, allowing two goals on nine shots. Rheaume went on to play for Atlanta in the International League and, on December 3, 1992, she became the first woman to play in a regular season pro game. In 1998, she was a member of Canada's first women's Olympic hockey team, silver medal winners at Nagano, Japan.

As the first woman to break into men's hockey, she has earned hundreds of thousands of dollars for being a pioneer: "I've had an interesting career. I've been involved in many wonderful hockey experiences, the best being signed by Phil Esposito and Tampa Bay."

Manon assembled and coached the first all-girls team – a Mission Betty team – to play in the famous Quebec City International Pee Wee Tournament in its forty-three years of existence.

From Hell's Kitchen to the Hall of Fame

Joe Mullen grew up in a place called Hell's Kitchen, a tough New York City neighborhood and a place where ice rinks were unheard of. But Joey loved hockey, so he learned how to play the game on roller skates. He was ten years old before he got his first pair of ice skates, and was able to try them out at Madison Square Garden, where his father Tom Mullen worked. Young Joe used discarded sticks from the New York Rangers dressing room. Joey idolized the great Ranger players of the day, men like Jean Ratelle, Vic Hadfield, and Rod Gilbert. He never dreamed he would someday surpass many of their records.

In time, Joe became a top college hockey player at Boston College. In his draft year, he was ignored by all the NHL teams. "Too slow, too small," the NHL scouts said. After college, he signed on as a free agent with the St. Louis Blues. The Blues soon discovered they owned a diamond in the rough.

Over the next seventeen years, Mullen scored 502 career goals, the most by any U.S.-born player. He averaged a point a game in 1062 games with four different clubs. He was the first American player to reach 1000 points and the first to score 500 goals. At age thirty-two, playing for Calgary, he became the second oldest player (after Johnny Bucyk) to score 50 goals in a season. He played a key role on three Stanley Cup winning teams – Calgary in 1989, and Pittsburgh in 1991 and 1992. And he captured two Lady Byng Trophies as hockey's most gentlemanly player. In November 2000, Mullen received hockey's highest honor – induction into the Hockey Hall of Fame.

The Player Who Wrestled Bears

When the Barnum and Bailey Circus toured North America years ago, a popular attraction was the bear-wrestling event. Such an event would be illegal today, but in the 1940s local tough guys would be invited to jump in a ring and try to pin a muzzled old brown bear. There would be a small reward for anyone who could put the creature on its back.

In Joliette, Quebec, a sixteen-year-old hockey player named Marcel Bonin flexed his biceps and leaped fearlessly into the ring. Young Bonin fought that muzzled monster to a draw. He may have failed to put the bruin on its back, but the good citizens of Joliette admired Bonin's grit and determination and applauded madly when the match was over.

Years later, Bonin revealed the secret to his success.

"The bear had been de-clawed, but still he must have weighed 400 pounds. But Marcel Bonin is not so dumb. I went to see that bear before the match. I fed him and played with him until we were pretty good friends. He was glad to see me when I jumped into the ring.

"I wrestled that same bear many times in the small towns in Quebec. Later, when I made it to the NHL with Detroit, a reporter called me a 'tough little bear wrestler from Quebec.'"

After a stint in Detroit, the bear wrestler was traded to the Montreal Canadiens, where he played on four Stanley Cup winning teams. One year, hoping to change his scoring luck, Bonin borrowed a pair of Rocket Richard's old gloves. "Maybe they'll help me get out of my slump," he told Richard. In the next eight games, Bonin scored eight goals.

Olympic Gold and Miracles on Ice

When the U.S. hockey team met Team Canada in the gold medal match at Salt Lake City in the 2002 Olympics, millions of American fans hoped that coach Herb Brooks could repeat the stunning victory he helped create in 1980, when his team of young collegians upset the mighty Soviet team and went on to win Olympic gold. But, unfortunately for Brooks, in 2002 it was Team Canada that defeated the U.S. 5–2, touching off a nation-wide celebration in Canada, a country that had thirsted for its own gold medal in hockey for fifty years.

The 1980 Winter Olympic Games in Lake Placid, New York, produced one of the greatest hockey upsets in the history of the Winter Olympics, an upset so unexpected, so stunning, that it became known as the Miracle on Ice.

The U.S. Olympic team was mostly an inexperienced group of college boys. Despite their unbeaten record in the tournament, nobody gave the Americans the slightest chance against the Soviets, gold medal winners at five straight Olympic Games and perennial World Champions.

"You were born to be hockey players," said head coach Herb Brooks to his players. "This is your moment." On February 22, 1980, the American kids skated out to face the mighty Soviet team. Goalie Jim Craig, whose record at Boston University was 29–4, came up with a spectacular performance – the game of his life. Midway through the third period, team captain Mike Eruzione slammed in what proved to be the winning goal in a 4–3 U.S. victory. The celebration began and swept across North America.

But the competition wasn't over, the gold medal not yet assured. There was a final match to be played against Finland.

Two days later, with millions of people watching on television, the young Americans captured the coveted gold medal by beating Finland 4–2. Against all odds, they had completed one of the most amazing upsets in Olympic hockey history.

Watson an Olympic Whiz

Harry "Moose" Watson was not like most hockey players. He never sought fame and fortune in the professional leagues. He was an amateur superstar who was born in Newfoundland but raised mostly in Winnipeg. There he became a well-known player in local hockey leagues before he left the game to serve overseas as a pilot in World War I.

Following his wartime service, in 1919–20 Watson led the Toronto Granite Club, OHA senior champions for three straight seasons, to the Allan Cup in 1922 and 1923.

When the Granites represented Canada at the first Winter Olympic Games in 1924 at Chamonix, France, European fans had never seen such a hockey powerhouse. Canada whipped Czechoslovakia 30–0, Sweden 22–0, and Switzerland 33–0 in the preliminary round. They scored eighty-five goals to none against. In the final round, the Granites walloped Great Britain 19–2, and the U.S. 6–1. In five matches, Moose Watson and his mates outscored their opponents 110 to 3. The flashiest individual on the team was Watson, who was unstoppable, scoring 36 goals in five games – an average of seven goals per game – as Canada easily won the Olympic title. In the 33–0 romp over Switzerland, Watson dazzled opponents and fans by scoring thirteen times.

On his return to Canada, Watson turned down all offers to play professional hockey, including a contract for $30,000 put forward by the Montreal Maroons. It would have made him the highest paid player in the NHL, receiving a salary comparable to a million dollars today. Even though he was never paid to play the game, Watson's amateur achievements were so impressive he was elected to the Hockey Hall of Fame in 1962.

Women in Hockey

When Team Canada defeated the U.S. women's team for the Olympic gold medal in 2002 at Salt Lake City, millions of TV viewers were thrilled by the individual skills and team play they witnessed. They might be surprised to learn that the number of women registering to play hockey has doubled and tripled in recent years. And little did they know that women's hockey has a fascinating history.

Lord Stanley's daughter Isobel was a player in 1890, taking part in games played on the outdoor rink next to Rideau Hall in Ottawa. Wearing long ankle-length dresses, women learned strategies that were foreign to males. They would crouch down in front of their goaltender, allowing the hems of their dresses to spread out along the ice. Opposing players found it difficult to shoot the puck through the mass of material.

In 1916, Albertine Lapansee of Cornwall was described as "the greatest woman player of all time." Huge crowds attended her games and she scored most of her team's goals. Suddenly, she moved to the United States. When she returned, she revealed she was a man. She called herself Albert Smith, opened a service station, and never played hockey again.

In 1955, Abigail Hoffman, posing as Ab Hoffman, played all season in an all-male league. Officials checked her birth certificate after she was selected for the all-star team – and discovered she was a girl. Abigail went on to become an Olympic athlete, not in hockey but as a track star.

Between 1930 and 1940, the Preston (Ontario) Rivulettes reigned as Canadian women's champions for ten straight years, winning all but two of 350 games played.

In 1998, the U.S. upset Canada to win the first gold medal in women's hockey at the Olympic Games in Nagano, Japan. The American women were expected to win a second gold medal against Canada in 2002, after compiling a thirty-five-game winning streak. But Canada, with Hayley Wickenheiser breaking a 2–2 tie, won the gold medal game over the U.S. with a score of 3–2, and skated off with the first Olympic gold for Team Canada – male or female – since 1952.

In Bala, Ontario, eighty-two-year-old Mickey Walker still plays recreational hockey once a week. She's registered as the world's oldest active female player.

Hazel McCallion, the Mayor of Mississauga, Ontario, now in her eighties, was one of the first known female professional players. Hazel received five dollars per game when she played in a Montreal league in the early 1940s.

The Oldest Rookie and Other Oldtimers

Veteran minor-league hockey star Connie Madigan waited a long time to see his hockey dream come true. On February 5, 1973, Madigan was brought up to the St. Louis Blues and played in his first NHL game. At the age of thirty-eight, Madigan became the oldest rookie in NHL history. He played in twenty regular season games and in five play-off games that season, scored no goals, and collected three assists. That same season, Boston introduced a rookie goaltender, thirty-six-year-old Ross Brooks, who promptly tied an NHL record with fourteen consecutive wins. But players older than Brooks and Madigan have performed in the NHL.

Minor league goalie Moe Roberts, after retiring from pro hockey in 1942, made a brief comeback in 1945–46, playing twenty-four games with a minor league club. He

later became a trainer for the Blackhawks. On November 24, 1951, Roberts strapped on the pads for one period of hockey in Chicago's 6–2 win over Detroit. He was almost forty-six years old and had last played in the NHL in 1933–34.

The Toronto Maple Leafs' Johnny Bower, who liked to keep his age a secret, was at least as old as Roberts when he retired from the NHL in 1970.

The most amazing oldtimer of them all was Gordie Howe, who was still playing in the NHL at age fifty-two. Howe was the league's only playing grandfather, and the only man who stayed around long enough to play on a line with his two sons in the NHL.

These Guys Were Durable

Can you imagine playing six hockey games in a row without taking a rest? In 1923, Ottawa star forward Frank Nighbor, who would eventually skate his way into the Hockey Hall of Fame, finished six full games without requiring a substitute. And during the streak, he scored six goals. Nighbor, from Pembroke, Ontario, was nicknamed The Pembroke Peach.

On March 20, 1996, goaltender Grant Fuhr of the St. Louis Blues displayed his durability. Fuhr became the first goalie in NHL history to start seventy-one games in one season, breaking a seventy-game record held by Eddie Johnston of Boston. Fuhr went on to play in seventy-nine games that season to establish a mark that still stands.

On April 5, 1987, forward Doug Jarvis completed his twelfth NHL season by playing in his 962nd consecutive game. He played in the first two games of the 1987–88 season before retiring, earning himself a place in the NHL record book with 964 consecutive games played.

A Hero at Every Game

He can't skate, has never scored a goal, goes around in circles, doesn't know the rules, and doesn't care who wins or loses. But players get out of his way when they see him coming. Everyone agrees – hockey wouldn't be the same without him. He is, of course, the Zamboni, the incredible ice-resurfacing machine, a rugged, reliable performer and the brainchild of the late Frank Zamboni.

A native of Utah, Frank Zamboni moved to California to work in his brother's garage. The brothers set up an ice-making plant and, when electric refrigerators killed the ice-making business, they decided to erect a skating rink. But when the arena opened, the Zamboni brothers found that resurfacing the ice required a lot of time and manpower. There had to be a better way to do the job.

In 1942, Frank Zamboni began to experiment with a mechanized vehicle to resurface the ice. The first machine he built was installed on a sled that was towed by a tractor, but it couldn't produce a smooth ice surface and didn't pick up the snow adequately. In 1949, Zamboni introduced a machine that could consistently create a good sheet of ice.

His invention caught the eye of the famous figure skater Sonja Henie, who was practicing at the Zamboni rink for her ice show. Miss Henie ordered a new machine and used it to make fresh ice on her nationwide tour. Wherever she appeared, rink operators watched in fascination as the Zamboni skimmed over the ice. Frank Zamboni began getting orders for more of his machines.

In the beginning, Zamboni's machine was known simply as "the ice machine." Then one night at a hockey game, some loudmouth fan yelled out: "Get the Zamboni out and make some new ice!" Others took up the chant and from then on the Zamboni name became a part of hockey.

The Zamboni first made an appearance at an NHL game on March 10, 1955, at the Montreal Forum.

Since the 1994 All Star Game in New York, two Zambonis have been used to resurface the ice between periods of NHL games.

Several years ago, a company called Jet Ice invented a purifying system for water used by Zambonis. Impurities in regular water rise to the surface, creating soft, chippy ice. The Jet Ice system results in a harder, more durable surface.

Zambonis have been seen in the popular comic strip *Peanuts*. Woodstock has one to prepare ice for his frozen birdbath, and Charlie Brown once said, "There are three things in life that are fun to watch: A rippling stream, a fire in the fireplace and a Zamboni going round and round and round . . ."

CHAPTER 5

HE SHOOTS, HE SCORES!

Five Goals in 42 Seconds!

Did you know that Bill Mosienko, a former star with the Chicago Blackhawks, once scored five times in less than a minute? Here's the catch – he did it over the course of two games played ten years apart.

Mosienko clearly holds the NHL record for hockey's three fastest goals, scored in 21 seconds. Those three he scored half a century ago on May 23, 1952, against rookie goaltender Lorne Anderson of the New York Rangers during the final game of the 1951–52 season. His center, Gus Bodnar, set a record for the three fastest assists in the same twenty-one-second span.

Those records are truly remarkable. But what has long been forgotten is that Mosienko – ten years earlier – scored a pair of goals against another Ranger goalie, "Sugar" Jim Henry, in a similar span of 21 seconds. It happened on February 8, 1942.

When you add it up, it comes to five goals in 42 seconds. No other scorer – not even Wayne Gretzky – has come close to matching Mosienko's mark.

Flukey Goals

During the 2002 winter Olympics, in a hockey game between Belarus and Sweden, Belarus scored a fascinating goal when the puck bounced off the head of Swedish goaltender Tommy Salo and spun into the net behind him.

During the 1988 Stanley Cup play-offs, the Calgary Flames' Al MacInnis scored a goal against Los Angeles while his team's trainer was out on the ice, attending to Calgary's injured goaltender.

A player in the American Hockey League, with his team leading 9–1, got a breakaway. As he darted in on goal, the goaltender stepped aside and said, "Be my guest," allowing the shooter to score into the empty net.

In the early 1900s, a goalie raced all the way down the ice to score a goal.

Another tale involving one of hockey's strangest goals can be found among some faded old newspaper clippings at the Hockey Hall of Fame in Toronto. The goal took everyone by surprise, and former NHL All Star Jack Adams was the man who scored it.

Adams was a star forward on the famed Vancouver Millionaires, a team that toiled in the Pacific Coast Hockey Association. In the final game of the 1920–21 season, Vancouver beat Victoria 11–8. During that high-scoring affair, Jack Adams accidentally scored a goal – on his own goaltender!

Since Adams' gaffe had no bearing on the game's outcome, his error was quickly forgotten. But it was noted by the official scorer at rinkside that night. The scorer, for reasons unknown, credited Adams for the goal and added it to his total in the individual scoring race. In fact, the goal against his own goalie vaulted him into fifth place in the scoring race. Later, Adams quipped, "If I'd known I'd get credit for a goal like that one, I might have been tempted to knock a few more pucks into our net. Heck, I could have won the scoring crown that way."

Ullman Makes His Mark

Hall of Fame center Norm Ullman was a solid two-way player – gifted offensively and defensively – for twenty NHL seasons. He scored 490 career goals for Detroit and Toronto. And while he never won a Stanley Cup, in 1965 Ullman established a play-off record for scoring that has never been broken – two goals in five seconds. And he scored the goals against Chicago's Glenn Hall, one of the greatest netminders in history.

"Glenn Hall was always hard to beat," Ullman recalls. "I'm amazed I could beat him twice in five seconds. Late in the second period I took a shot from well out, maybe forty to fifty feet. The puck caught the goalpost and went in. Then, right off the face-off, I intercepted a pass and took another long shot. This time a defenseman screened my shot and I saw the red light flash. The goals came at 17:35 and 17:40. After the game, someone came into our dressing room and told me I'd set a record for the fastest two play-off goals. I recall thinking nobody beats Glenn Hall twice in five seconds."

Ullman was a Detroit Red Wing for more than eleven seasons and led the Wings in scoring three times. He was traded to Toronto a year after the Maple Leafs won the Stanley Cup in 1967. Norm Ullman was inducted into the Hockey Hall of Fame in 1982.

He Led Three NHL Clubs in Scoring

There was little doubt that center Vincent Damphousse, a scoring star with the Laval Junio rs in the early 1980s, was going to be an outstanding NHL player. But none of the scouts who saw him play would have predicted he would someday lead three NHL clubs in scoring – in consecutive seasons.

Until Damphousse came along, drafted sixth overall by the Toronto Maple Leafs in 1986, no player in NHL history had performed such an unusual feat. In his fifth season in Toronto in 1990–91, Damphousse led the Maple Leafs in scoring with 73 points. The following season, he was traded to the Edmonton Oilers, where he collected a team high of 89 points. Another off-season trade sent him to the Montreal Canadiens, and once again he topped all his teammates with 97 points. The only other player to lead three different teams in scoring, but not in consecutive years, is retired pro Lanny McDonald, who was his team's scoring leader in Toronto, Colorado, and Calgary.

A Record Night for Sittler

When the Boston Bruins faced the Toronto Maple Leafs at Maple Leaf Gardens on the night of February 7, 1976, Boston coach Don Cherry had a problem. Who would be his starting goaltender? Would it be Dave Reece, the rookie who had won seven of fourteen starts? Or should he gamble on veteran Gerry Cheevers, who had just jumped back to the Bruins from the Cleveland Crusaders of the World Hockey Association? He went with Reece. For Dave Reece, the game that night would be a nightmare, and Leafs captain Darryl Sittler would be responsible for most of his suffering.

In the first period, Sittler assisted on two Leafs goals. But he really started to fly in the second, setting up two more goals and scoring three times himself. Seven points for the captain and still a third period to play. In the final twenty minutes, he scored three more goals – that's two hat tricks in two periods!

Sittler's ten point game – six goals and four assists – added up to the greatest individual scoring performance in NHL history, and no player has matched it yet. The Leafs won the game 11–4. Sittler not only shattered records, he helped destroy the NHL career of Dave Reece. His confidence in tatters, Reece never played another NHL game.

Hill's Half-a-Puck Goal

In 1902, the Toronto Wellingtons embarked on a long train ride west to Winnipeg where they challenged the Winnipeg Victorias for the Stanley Cup.

The Wellingtons were missing a player because the parents of the youngest player on the team refused to let him go. In the first game of the three-game series, one of the players on the ice hoisted the puck high in the air and it became lodged in the rafters over the ice. There was a delay until one of the players threw his stick skyward and knocked the puck free. Apparently a replacement puck could not be found. Then snow slipped through the cracks in the roof of the Winnipeg Arena and formed little lines along the ice. Later, a big dog jumped on the ice and play was halted while ushers tried to chase it off.

During one of the games, a Toronto player named Chummy Hill was startled to see the puck split in two while he fought for possession of it. The broken puck lay directly in front of the Winnipeg goal. Hill reacted by cradling one of the pieces with his stick and shooting it into the Winnipeg net. The referee ruled Hill's shot a goal despite a wild protest from the Winnipeg players. Chummy Hill remains the only player in Stanley Cup history to score a goal with half a puck. But even if Chummy had whacked both halves of the puck in the net, it wouldn't have been enough. Winnipeg won the two-game series by scores of 5–3 and 5–3.

The Broken-Back Goal

During a game in Boston in 1964, winger Dean Prentice of the Boston Bruins, racing in on the Chicago goal on a breakaway, was hauled down from behind by Stan Mikita of the Blackhawks. Prentice crashed heavily into the end boards and lay there semi-conscious.

The Bruins star was unaware that the referee had awarded him a penalty shot on the play until he was helped to his feet by his teammates. He complained of feeling ill and there was numbness in his back. Even though he was still groggy, Prentice took the penalty shot – and scored. Moments later, sitting on the Boston bench, his legs and back began to tighten up, and he couldn't stand up. He called for help, saying he felt paralyzed. Prentice was rushed to a nearby hospital where doctors diagnosed a fractured vertebra – a broken back! It was a serious injury, one that kept him out of action for a long time. But it didn't stop Dino from scoring a penalty shot goal before he was removed from the game.

An Impossible Shot

Dave Duncan will be the first to tell you he wasn't much of a hockey player. He never expected to be the guy people count on to score the big goal, to make the winning play. So when the twenty-five-year-old from Oshawa, Ontario, attempted to win $8000 toward the purchase of a new car in one of those hockey Score-O competitions between periods, he wasn't given much of a chance.

Dave Duncan could barely envision the end of the rink, much less the tiny slot at the base of the board covering the goal net. Aside from being legally blind, Duncan was faced with the near-impossible task of shooting a 3" puck three-quarters of the way down the ice surface and through that tiny slot, just slightly wider than the puck itself. But Duncan was determined to try. He amazed onlookers by sending a perfectly aimed shot through the hole and into the net. It was a one-in-a-million shot and Duncan delivered it.

Eye in the Sky

For the first time in NHL history, a video replay was required to determine the outcome of a play-off game. It happened during the 1992 Division semi-final play-off series between Detroit and Minnesota. In overtime, Sergei Federov of the Red Wings took a high shot that appeared to hit the crossbar. After a stop in play, referee Rob Shick consulted the supervisor of officials and video-replay judge Wally Harris. Both men determined that the puck had entered the net, giving the Red Wings a 1–0 victory.

A few years later, when players were forbidden to enter the goalie's crease, the video-replay judge played an important role in the outcome of the 1999 Stanley Cup finals between Buffalo and Dallas. Game six went to three overtime periods before Brett Hull scored the winning goal and the Dallas Stars skated off with the Cup. But replays showed

that Hull clearly had one foot in the crease when he stuffed the puck past Sabres goalie Dominik Hasek. Long after the game, NHL spokesman Bryan Lewis stated there had been a review of Hull's disputed goal and it had been allowed to stand because "Hull had possession of the puck when his left foot entered the crease." Buffalo fans didn't buy the explanation. They hadn't seen it that way. But there was nothing they could do about it.

The Goal of the 20th Century

If asked to name the greatest goal ever scored, most Canadian hockey fans would pick Paul Henderson's famous goal, the one that sank the Soviets back in September 1972. It's often been called The Goal of Century – the 20th century.

It happened in Moscow in the deciding game of the incredibly exciting eight-game series between Team Canada and the Soviets. After trailing in the series by three games to one (with one game tied), Team Canada fought back on Russian ice to deadlock the series with one game left to play.

What many fans don't know about that series-clinching goal by Paul Henderson is that he almost wasn't around to score it. At least one doctor had suggested that he should sit out what would be the most important game of his life. In the previous game, in which he also scored the game-winning goal, he had tumbled into the boards, striking his head. He was still feeling groggy on the eve of the final match.

"Why not sit out?" the doctor asked. "Why risk further injury?"

"No way," said Paul. "I've got a strong feeling that game eight might be a game in which I can do something special."

It was a decision he would never regret. In the final twenty minutes of the game, when all appeared to be lost, Team Canada fought back with two third-period goals to tie the score at five. Then, with seconds ticking down in the final minute of play, Paul raced to the net and was tripped. He flew into the end boards, bounced up, and moved right in front of Tretiak, the young Russian goaltender.

Just then, from the face-off circle to the right of Tretiak, Phil Esposito whirled and took a shot on goal, hitting Tretiak. The rebound came right to Henderson's stick. With just over half a minute left on the clock, he shot once, got a rebound, then shot again. On his second try he flipped the puck expertly into the Soviet net. There were 34 seconds left to play. Team Canada held on to win the game 6–5.

Three decades later, Paul Henderson is stopped almost daily wherever he goes. People ask for his autograph and tell him where they were and what they were doing at the very moment he scored his memorable goal. They all remember the man who scored the goal of the century.

CHAPTER 6
STRANGE BUT TRUE

The Mystery of the Missing Nose

When young Ivan Matulik, a Czech native, arrived in North America several years ago to play for the Halifax Citadels of the American Hockey League, he knew his life was about to change. What he didn't anticipate was losing part of his nose.

The incident happened during the 1991–92 season on a road trip, and it happened so fast Ivan couldn't believe it. He collided with an opposing player, who fell awkwardly. The blade of his opponent's skate blade flew past Ivan's face and neatly sliced off part of his nose. Blood flowed as Ivan left the ice to be treated by the team trainer and the opposing team's doctor. He was shocked to learn that part of his nose was missing. Could it be found? And could it be re-attached?

By this time the period was over. The Zamboni was cleaning the ice. It had already passed over the spot where the accident occurred. There was only one place the missing piece of nose could be – somewhere inside the Zamboni, somewhere in all that slush and snow. When the Zamboni dumped its chilly load, a frantic search began. Within minutes, the searchers were rewarded when one of them triumphantly held up a small piece of flesh.

Ivan Matulik and the tip of his nose were rushed to hospital where surgeons skillfully re-attached it. Fortunately, the nose tip had been well preserved by ice and snow after the accident.

Within a few months, Ivan's nose had healed and looked perfectly normal. A doctor examined the wound and asked him how it had happened. Ivan said, "Hockey." The doctor said, "That figgers."

Hockey and Football Switch Stadiums

Two U.S. college teams, the University of Michigan and Michigan State, played a hockey game before the largest crowd in hockey history. The unique event, which was played outdoors, took place on the football field at Spartan Stadium in Lansing, Michigan. The game was played on the afternoon on October 6, 2001, and was witnessed by 74,544 cheering fans.

It cost about $500,000 to install a temporary ice pad on the football field and weather conditions were ideal for the game, which was six years in the planning. Both coaches, Red Berenson of Michigan and Ron Mason of Michigan State, said they were pleased with the result, a 3–3 tie.

Hall of Fame member Gordie Howe, who resides in Michigan, dropped the puck for the ceremonial face-off and said, "When I was a boy, all of my hockey was played outdoors. This is a piece of history. The players will never forget it."

Why would National Football League officials decide to hold their league's first title game inside a hockey rink? On December 18, 1932, when a blizzard dumped several inches of snow on the city of Chicago, they had little choice. That's why the championship game of the newly formed National Football League was played indoors, in the Chicago Stadium, home of the Blackhawks.

Stadium officials cooperated and workers pushed rinkside seats back several inches. Trucks dumped a layer of soil over the floor of the arena. The soil was trampled down and crude line markings were painted over it. By game time the "field" – not quite regulation size – was ready for play. The turnstiles opened, and more than 11,000 fans came in from the snow to witness one of the most unique sports events in Chicago history – a championship game between the Chicago Bears and the Portsmouth (Ohio) Spartans.

Because the playing surface was only 80 instead of the regulation 100 yards long, every time a team crossed midfield it was set back 20 yards. Following their 9–0 defeat, the Spartans pulled up stakes and moved to Detroit where they became the Detroit Lions. If the Spartans are remembered at all, it's for being shutout in a football championship game played in a hockey rink.

The Longest Game Ever

Have you ever played in a hockey game where both teams scored over 300 goals? Or a game where the top scorer came through with sixty goals? If so, you must have been one of 180 players who showed up to compete in the first annual Labatt Blue/NHL Pickup Marathon held in Toronto from January 31 through February 3, 2000.

Two teams of ninety players – Blues and Whites – competed in ninety-eight periods of play stretching over 71 hours and 52 minutes. The Blues blew a 237–215 lead and lost 380–340, according to several busy statisticians at rinkside.

The event was held on the open-air skating rink at Nathan Phillips Square across from Toronto City Hall. Each team comprised five squads of fifteen to eighteen skaters and three goaltenders. When a team grew weary, it skated off and was replaced by a fresh team. The final group lasted the longest, playing for about twenty hours. The leading scorer in the unique event was Brett Punchard, a former college player at Bowling Green University in Ohio. He racked up 37 goals and 60 points over twenty-six periods in the marathon. Labatt donated five dollars for every minute played to the Hockey Fights Cancer fund – a total contribution of about $10,000.

The Shortest Game Ever

Rugged defenseman John Brophy was overjoyed to team up on defense with Don Perry when both played for the Long Island Ducks in the old Eastern Hockey League. They soon terrorized the entire league with their crash and bash style. One game in which Brophy and Perry played lasted all of eighty seconds.

The New Haven Blades were the visitors that night, and when Brophy and Perry assaulted the Blades with sticks and fists on the very first shift, that was enough. The Blades left the ice, showered quickly, threw on their street clothes, and began to hurry out of the dressing room.

Al Baron, owner of the Ducks, ran down to intercept the Blades in their dash for safety. Baron realized he would lose a lot of money if the game was canceled or forfeited. In the visitor's dressing room, he flashed a roll of bills. "I'm offering each of you a hundred dollars to go back on the ice," he pleaded. The Blades replied, "No thanks, Al, we'd be crazy to go back on the ice with those two gorillas waiting there to kill us."

Baron reluctantly had to make refunds to all the fans. And when he spoke to Perry and Brophy about their aggressive play, one of them said, "Gee, Al, what are those Blades beefing about? We didn't do anything tonight we haven't been doing all season long."

The Substitute Linesmen Were Players

A blizzard swept down from Canada and buried New England in snow. Referee Dan Marouelli and linesman Ron Fournier were en route to Hartford for a Whalers–Islanders game, and they knew they were going to be late getting there. With luck, they might arrive partway through the game. But who would don the striped shirts if they didn't get to Hartford?

Ron Foyt, the second linesman appointed to the game, was already at the arena in Hartford. When the other two officials didn't show up by game time, he knew he couldn't handle the game all by himself. He needed help.

He skimmed through the NHL rule book and found exactly what he was looking for. Under the rules, if Foyt took over as referee, he was permitted to recruit a player from each club to serve as linesmen in the game. He had no trouble finding volunteers. Gary Howatt of the New York Islanders and Mickey Vulcan of the Hartford Whalers were both nursing minor injuries. But both could skate and both were willing to assist Foyt because it was the opportunity of a lifetime.

So the game was played and the first period went by without a hitch. During the intermission, Fournier and Marouelli finally arrived and replaced the two players who had helped create an NHL first. Howatt and Vulcan are the only two modern-day players ever to act as game officials in the NHL.

Referee in a Basket

Frank Carlin, a hockey manager from Montreal, took his senior team to Boston one weekend. When his team arrived at the arena and stepped on the ice for the warm up, there didn't appear to be a referee for the match.

"I asked the two linesmen about it," he said. "They laughed and pointed up toward the rafters in the arena.

"'The referee's up there – sitting in a basket,' they said.

"Sure enough, high over the ice was the referee. He even waved down at me. And that's where he stayed for the entire game. It seemed that somebody thought the official would have a better view of the action if he was perched high above the ice surface.

"The experiment didn't last. It was a ridiculous idea. Both teams had a devil of a time understanding his penalty calls. Still, it's the only time in my hockey career I'd seen such a thing."

Sutton Outscored Gretzky

It wasn't often that Wayne Gretzky was outshone or overshadowed by an opponent in a hockey game. That was especially true in minor hockey, where Wayne scored goals like no other minor player in history, collecting goal number 1000 by the time he was a teen. But there was one game that left Wayne shedding tears in the dressing room. Gretzky had scored a goal and collected three assists in the game – a fine effort – but Grove Sutton, a star player on the opposing team, had done even better.

It was 1974 and the event was the 15th Annual Quebec International Pee Wee Hockey Tournament. Gretzky was the biggest story at the tournament, and more than 10,000 fans turned out to see him play. In Brantford's opening 25–0 win against a nervous group of youngsters from Richardson, Texas, Gretzky scored 7 goals and added 4 assists for 11 points, breaking Guy Lafleur's single-game tournament record by one. He followed up with two goals and three assists in Brantford's 9–1 victory over Beaconsfield, Quebec. Game three was against Verdun, Quebec, a team featuring a flashy centerman named Denis Savard who would go on to a Hall-of-Fame career in the NHL. Brantford won again, 7–3, with Wayne notching three goals.

Brantford's next test – in the tournament semi-finals – was against a team from Oshawa, Ontario, a club with speed and depth and a kid named Grove Sutton. Wayne played well, but Oshawa's smooth-skating little star overshadowed him, scoring five times in a 9–4 Oshawa victory. Sutton wasn't just a one-game wonder, for he collected 17 goals in the tournament, four more than Gretzky. Sutton's future looked bright. Few would have thought that he would soon fade from the hockey scene, to be remembered only by the fans who saw him outshine Wayne Gretzky, the most dynamic young player in the game.

CHAPTER 7
THE STANLEY CUP

The Original Stanley Cup

The Stanley Cup is the oldest team trophy competed for in North America. It has been battered and kicked around, lost and stolen, held high in triumph and kissed by thousands of lips.

In 1893, when Canada's Governor General, Lord Stanley of Preston, decided to donate a trophy to the "championship team of the Dominion," he had a small silver bowl imported from England. The bowl was about the size of a football and cost about fifty dollars. Unfortunately, Lord Stanley never saw the cup named after him being won; he returned to England before the first Cup game was played. He holds the unique position of being a member of the Hockey Hall of Fame without ever seeing a play-off game.

Legend has it that an Ottawa star, on a dare one night, kicked the Stanley Cup into the Rideau Canal. It was found the next morning, stuck in the ice and snow covering the frozen canal.

In 1924, the Cup was almost lost again. A group of Montreal players, on their way to a victory party, had to stop their car to fix a flat tire. They deposited the Stanley Cup on the sidewalk while the tire was being replaced. The players continued their journey and arrived at the party – without the Cup! They dashed back to the scene of the tire change and there was the Cup, sitting right where they had left it.

Guy Lafleur once kidnapped the Stanley Cup after a Canadiens victory party and took it to his home town of Thurso, Quebec. A decade ago, it wound up in Mario Lemieux's swimming pool after a Pittsburgh Penguins Cup victory, and it has even been on display in Moscow.

If the Stanley Cup could talk, it would have some wonderful stories to tell, including the time when the baby son of Hall of Famer Red Kelly was lifted into the bowl of the cup to have his photo taken. Can you imagine what the infant did in there? Red says, "Good thing he had a thick diaper on!"

Worst Goalie in Cup History Was Just a Kid

Picture this. A seventeen-year-old goalie approaches his parents. The year is 1904, the place is Dawson City in the Yukon.

"Mom and Dad," the boy says, "I've been asked to play goal for the local hockey team when they challenge for the Stanley Cup. Can I go?"

"I don't know," says the boy's father. "Where will the games be played?"

"In Ottawa."

"That's about 4000 miles away. How are you getting there, son?"

"We're planning to leave on our bicycles for Whitehorse. That's about 350 miles down the trail. Some of the guys will be walking, and a couple may go by dogsled. From Whitehorse we'll take the train to Skagway in Alaska. After that we'll go by steamship to

Vancouver. Then we'll get back on the train and go to Ottawa. It may take us a month to get there."

"Hmmm, that's mighty long way to go just to play hockey, son. You'll miss a lot of school. And what's this Stanley Cup thing all about, anyway?"

"It's a trophy, Dad. Any old team can challenge for it and every team wants to win it. We think out can win it for Dawson City. Can I go?"

"Oh, I don't see why not," says the father.

"Just behave yourself and don't get hurt," says the mother. "When will you be back, son?"

"I have no idea. But sometime in 1905."

A discussion just like this one must have happened in December 1904, just before seventeen-year-old Albert Forrest left with his teammates for a Stanley Cup series against the Ottawa Silver Seven. The Dawson City players arrived in Ottawa without having practiced for almost a month. They lost by scores of 9–2 and 23–2, and in one of the games, Ottawa star Frank McGee scored 14 goals against young Forrest. But most agreed if it hadn't been for Forrest's plucky play, the Ottawa snipers might have doubled their goal production. McGee's 14 goals in one game remains an all-time Stanley Cup scoring record. After more than a century of play-off games for the Stanley Cup, Albert Forrest remains the youngest, and the most porous, of all play-off goaltenders.

Can you imagine the conversation when Albert got home?

"Hi, Mom. Hi, Dad. It's good to be home again."

"Hello, son. I'm glad you made it back all right," says Mr. Forrest.

"Hi, Albert. I think you've grown an inch," says Mrs. Forrest.

"I hear you lost both games," says the father.

"We did. And a fellow named McGee scored fourteen times against me – in one game. He was lucky."

"Oh, well, there's always next year."

"No, Dad. They said we wouldn't be invited back next year."

The Cup Series Was Abandoned

Only once has a final series for the Stanley Cup not been fought to a conclusion. It happened in the spring of 1919, during a close battle for the Cup between the Seattle Metropolitans and the Montreal Canadiens.

In game five, played in Seattle, the players on both teams appeared to be skating in slow motion. Most of them were suffering from symptoms of a serious flu epidemic which had been sweeping across North America, killing thousands of people. Some of the feverish players staggered off their benches and fell down on the ice. Montreal's toughest player, Bad Joe Hall, collapsed and could not get up. Half unconscious, he was rushed to a nearby hospital.

The manager of the Canadiens offered to bring in players from the Victoria team for the next game, to replace the Montreal players who were ill, but Seattle turned down the proposal.

The Stanley Cup trustees had no choice but to cancel the rest of the series. The Canadiens left by train for home while their star, Joe Hall, remained in hospital in critical condition. Hall passed away a few days later.

Clancy Could Play Anywhere

Hall of Fame defenseman Frank "King" Clancy, who scored his first NHL goal by shooting the puck through a hole in the side of the net instead of through the front opening, holds another unique niche in NHL history. He's the only player to play every position for his team in a game. And he did it in a Stanley Cup play-off match.

In the 1923 play-offs, the Ottawa Senators journeyed west by train to Vancouver, where they were challenged by not one, but two teams for the Stanley Cup. If the Senators defeated Vancouver in one series, they would then face Edmonton in another. The Senators found the first task to be an easy one. They disposed of the Vancouver Maroons in four games.

The Edmonton team was standing by, fully expecting to win. The Senators had suffered a number of injuries against the Maroons and half their roster was on the limp. In one of the games against Edmonton, Clancy was told he would have to fill in wherever he was needed. He played both left and right defense and all three forward positions. "If the referee gets hurt, I guess I could take over for him as well." Clancy quipped.

Moments later, goalie Clint Benedict of the Senators was given a penalty. During that era, penalized goalies had to serve their time in the penalty box. When Benedict skated to the box he tossed his goal stick to Clancy and said, "Let's see if you can defend my goal until I get back." Clancy was up to the challenge and played in goal for two minutes.

"I didn't do much, but I wasn't scored on," he would say, rather proudly. "And we went on to win the game and the Cup." Clancy's brief stint in goal made him the only player in history to play all six positions in a Stanley Cup game.

Hockey's Longest Play-off Game

In more than a century of Stanley Cup games, there have been some memorable overtime games played. But none compares with an extra-period game played at the Montreal Forum almost seventy years ago.

It was March 24, 1936, when the Detroit Red Wings and the Montreal Maroons clashed in the first round of the play-offs. The teams began their game at 8:34 p.m., but they wouldn't finish the match until 2:25 the following morning – in the sixth overtime period.

The scoreless battle lasted almost six hours and was finally settled by an unlikely hero, a twenty-one-year-old Detroit rookie named Modere (Mud) Bruneteau. Bruneteau had scored a mere two goals during the regular season, but as the marathon game wore on he got more and more ice time because of his boundless energy. While older players were gasping as one overtime period followed another, Bruneteau's young legs remained strong.

Then, at the 16:30 mark of the sixth overtime, he got a break. Taking a pass from Hec Kilrea, Bruneteau deked Montreal goalie Lorne Chabot and slipped in the only goal of the game.

Hockey's longest play–off game was finally over and Mud Bruneteau ended it. It's one hockey record that may never be broken.

Bill Barilko's Last Shot

A handsome young defenseman played a starring role in a memorable Stanley Cup final series, a torrid battle in 1951 between the Montreal Canadiens and the Toronto Maple Leafs. All five games in the series were settled in overtime – a post-season first. Bill Barilko was the Maple Leafs defenseman who dashed in to score the series-winning goal for his team, ending the season.

With the Leafs holding a lead of three games to one in the series, game five was played at Maple Leaf Gardens. The Habs fought hard to prolong the series and held a 2–1 lead late in the third period. With time running out, Leafs coach Joe Primeau pulled his goalie. It proved to be a wise move because Tod "Slinker" Sloan tied the score with just 32 seconds on the clock, beating goalie Gerry McNeil and forcing yet another overtime.

Early in the overtime, Howie Meeker passed the puck from behind the Montreal net to an onrushing Bill Barilko. As he slapped the puck past a startled McNeil for the Stanley Cup-winning goal, Barilko's skates left the ice. He flew through the air – an image captured on film by a rinkside photographer in one of hockey's most dramatic photos.

A few weeks later, Barilko and a friend disappeared on a fly-in fishing trip in northern Ontario. Despite a month-long search covering hundreds of miles and costing thousands of dollars, the crash site of the small plane in which Barilko and his friend died was not discovered for another eleven years.

Stop That Thief – He's Stolen the Cup!

From 1956 through 1960, the Montreal Canadiens captured the Stanley Cup a record five times straight. Their dynasty was finally brought to a halt by Bobby Hull, Stan Mikita, Glenn Hall, and the rest of the Chicago Blackhawks in the 1961 Stanley Cup play-offs.

The Hawks and the Habs met in a semi-final series the following year, and midway through a game at the Chicago Stadium, with Chicago goalie Glenn Hall playing superbly, it became obvious that Chicago was going to win the series, four games to two, and move on to the finals against Toronto.

In the crowd, a staunch Montreal fan named Ken Kilander watched in dismay. It was intolerable to think any team but Montreal could hold Lord Stanley's famous trophy. Impulsively, Kilander jumped up from his seat and raced down to the lobby of the Chicago stadium. There was the coveted Stanley Cup, on display inside a locked showcase. Boldly, Kilander smashed the case, grabbed the famous trophy, and darted toward an exit. An alarm sounded. Stadium ushers and police chased after Kilander. The thief didn't get very far before he was apprehended and arrested.

The following morning, Kilander tried to explain his actions to a judge.

"Your honor, I was simply taking the Cup back to Montreal where it belongs," he said.

"This is going to be Chicago's year to win the Cup," snapped the judge. "But you belong in Montreal, Mr. Kilander, and you'd better get back there before I lock you up and throw away the key."

Lights Out at the Boston Garden

The Edmonton Oilers and the Boston Bruins were locked in a 3–3 tie at the Boston Garden. It was May 24, 1988, the fourth game of the Stanley Cup finals, and 14,500 frantic fans screamed their support for the hometown Bruins. Suddenly the screaming stopped and the crowd was hushed. With 3:23 left to play in the second period, an overload on a 4000-volt switch knocked out the lights in the rundown old building, leaving players, referees, and fans in the dark.

After a long delay, an auxiliary generator provided some light, but not enough to play by. Officials ordered the building evacuated and NHL president John Ziegler declared that the game would be replayed in its entirety, two nights later in Edmonton. With the unexpected home-ice advantage, the Oilers breezed to a 6–3 victory over the Bruins and captured their fourth Stanley Cup in five years.

Yzerman Shows Class

In late August 1997, Detroit Red Wings captain Steve Yzerman, a future Hall of Famer, brought the Stanley Cup to Ottawa. To be more accurate, he brought it to the suburb of Nepean, where he played minor hockey and where he once led a Pee Wee team to the provincial championship.

Carrying the famous silver trophy, Yzerman walked along the red carpet where he was greeted by a couple of thousand people gathered in the new Steve Yzerman Arena.

In the crowd that day was another Steve – an old friend named Steve Unger. As a teenager, Unger had played hockey with great skill. He played center like Yzerman, and displayed unlimited potential. Both Steves were destined to become stars in the NHL. But in 1984, there was a tragic accident. Sixteen-year-old Unger went swimming in the Ottawa River. He dove into shallow water and suffered a broken neck, an injury that would leave him paralyzed, a quadriplegic. Following the accident, Yzerman and former Nepean goalie Darren Pang set up a trust fund for their crippled pal.

In the arena that day, Yzerman spotted Unger in the crowd. Without hesitating, the longest-serving captain in NHL history made his way through the crowd to the smiling man in the wheelchair. Gently Yzerman placed the Stanley Cup in Unger's lap. Tears welled up in Unger's eyes as the crowd cheered and applauded. Steve Yzerman, hockey icon, and Steve Unger, who might have become one, shared a very emotional moment.

CHAPTER 8

BETWEEN THE PIPES

Raw Recruit Becomes Play-off MVP

The soft spoken, articulate young man was a star goaltender – an All American – in U.S. college hockey at Cornell University. In three seasons of college play, Toronto native Ken Dryden won seventy-six of eighty-three games played. Drafted by the Boston Bruins in 1964, his pro rights were traded to Montreal. Late in the 1970–71 season, the Habs brought Dryden up to the NHL and coach Scotty Bowman gave him a half-dozen starts – Dryden won every game he played.

When the Canadiens opened the play-offs, they were pitted against the powerful Boston Bruins, led by superstars Bobby Orr and Phil Esposito. The Bruins had established several records on their way to a first-place finish, and were stunned to see Ken Dryden – a raw rookie – start in goal for Montreal. As expected, Boston raced out to a 5–1 lead. Suddenly, in period two, the Canadiens began to fight back. They scored a goal, then another, then four more to take a 7–5 lead. The Bruins regrouped for a third-period assault on Dryden, but the lanky goaltender turned aside shot after shot. And when the final buzzer sounded, he had won his first play-off game. The Canadiens eventually eliminated the Bruins in seven games. Phil Esposito, who had scored a record 76 goals during the regular season, couldn't believe the rookie goalie had held him to just three goals in the series.

The Canadiens went on to eliminate the Chicago Blackhawks in the final series for the Stanley Cup, and Dryden played a key role in the victory. At season's end he was awarded the Conn Smythe Trophy as Most Valuable Player of the play-offs, a remarkable achievement for an inexperienced newcomer. The following season, Dryden skated off with the Calder Trophy as the league's top freshman. No player in history had been a play-off MVP one season and a rookie award winner the next.

Dryden helped the Habs win six Stanley Cups and was inducted into the Hockey Hall of Fame in 1983. He is now the President of the Toronto Maple Leafs.

The Gambling Goalie

In the early 1970s, goalie Ed Johnston of the Boston Bruins, following one of his best seasons, sought a raise in pay to $20,000 a year. But the Bruins executive vice president Charles Mulcahy scoffed at the idea, saying he didn't think Johnston's work in goal was worth such a fabulous salary. When the executive and the player couldn't reach an greement, Mulcahy, a scratch golfer, challenged Johnston to a golf match – three holes of golf for the raise. "If you can beat me, Eddie," he said, "you'll get your raise. Honest."

But Johnston was a capable golfer, too. And he liked to gamble.

"Let's make the stakes double or nothing," the goalie suggested. "If I win, you'll double my current salary. If I lose, there'll be no raise."

"You're on," laughed Mulcahy. "And we'll play on my course."

On the day of the match, Johnston's drives were long and straight, his putting was superb, and he beat his boss over the three holes they played. Mulcahy took his loss like the sportsman he was, praising his goaltender's play and doubling his pay.

Later in his career, Johnston would become a hockey executive. As general manager of the Pittsburgh Penguins, he signed Mario Lemieux to his first contract. But he didn't dare suggest settling Mario's salary on the golf course. For he knew that Mario's prowess as a golfer almost matched his skills on the hockey rink.

She Filled the Net

Many years ago, the University of Toronto women's hockey team had many fine stick-handlers and defense players – but no goalie. The skaters finally solved their problem by approaching the biggest girl on campus. After much persuasion she agreed to fill the position, but confessed she had no idea how to skate. "Welcome to the club anyway," said the other girls. "We'll teach you."

It wasn't an easy task. Finding skates large enough for their towering new recruit proved difficult. And fitting her into them took time and energy. Before each game, her teammates helped her into her equipment, propelled her across the ice, and propped her up between the goal posts.

"Promise me I won't have to stop a lot of pucks," pleaded the rookie.

"You'll be fine," said her teammates. "We'll give you lots of help."

And they kept their word. In one game, the awkward novice made three stops. In each of two other games, she made two stops. In another game she turned aside one puck, and in the remaining two games she made no stops at all, for there were no pucks directed her way.

Her goalposts became her biggest supporters, and she hugged them tenaciously. Her teammates spent most of each intermission getting her on and off the ice. It was hard work but well worth it. By the end of the season, the big goalie possessed a sparkling goals-against average and was proud to accept her crest as a member of the championship team.

"Hockey is fun, but this is it for me," she announced after the final game. "I'm going to quit while I'm ahead."

She left the arena and never came back.

Two Goalies in the Same Net

In one early-day Stanley Cup play-off game, a team from Rat Portage (now Kenora), Ontario, unveiled a bit of novel hockey strategy. When they played for the Stanley Cup against the powerful Ottawa team, the coach decided to put two goalies in the net – at the same time! Ottawa officials said he couldn't do that, and he replied, "Why not? I've checked the rule book and there's not a thing in there to prevent me."

The officials checked the rule book and grudgingly admitted he was right. So the Rat Portage coach took a player from his forward line and told him he would be the "extra" netminder.

The two goalies created a hubbub among the spectators when they rubbed elbows in the goal. To the Ottawa players, they looked formidable. There didn't appear to be any room to get a puck past them. But after a few rushes, the Ottawa boys discovered they had nothing to fear. The two goalies were hapless. They stumbled into each other and knocked each other off balance when they tried to block shots. Their sticks got tangled up and they fell down a lot. Ottawa won the game easily and the two goalie experiment was quickly abandoned. "I thought it might work, but it didn't," the innovative coach said with a shrug.

Tugnutt Stops Seventy Shots

Goalie Ron Tugnutt of the Quebec Nordiques might have suspected he was in for a long evening when he faced the hard-shooting Boston Bruins on the night of March 21, 1991. After all, he was about to face renowned shooters like Cam Neely and Ray Bourque. Tugnutt expected to be busy, but he didn't expect to be under a constant barrage.

From the opening face-off, the Bruins started peppering him with shots at a rate of more than a shot every minute. But Tugnutt, with acrobatic moves, denied the Bruins at least a dozen goals. At the end of regulation time, the score was tied 3–3. In the overtime, Tugnutt put on a display of goaltending that brought the Bruins fans to their feet. They had no love for the rest of the Quebec players, but Tugnutt became their pet.

With seconds left to play in the overtime frame, Tugnutt robbed both Bourque and Neely of goals with outstanding saves, preserving the tie and a single point for his team. When the final buzzer sounded, the exhausted netminder had stopped 70 of 73 shots. As the crowd stood and gave him a thunderous ovation, Cam Neely skated up to the exhausted Tugnutt and said, "Take a bow, pal. It's you they're applauding tonight."

Many in the crowd assumed the 73 shots on Tugnutt was a league record. Not so. The mark for most shots in a game is held by a former Chicago Blackhawks netminder, Sam Lopresti, who was bombarded by 83 Boston shots in a game played fifty years earlier, almost to the day. Incredibly, Lopresti almost stole a win for the Hawks that night, finally losing 3–2.

The patriotic Lopresti joined the U.S. Navy shortly afterward, saying, "It may be safer facing Nazi U-boats in the Atlantic than dodging hockey pucks in the NHL." Ironically, he had plenty of time to consider that sentiment when his ship was torpedoed and he managed to survive for forty-five days adrift on a life raft.

Brimsek's Debut One for the Books

In 1938, Boston Bruins fans were outraged when manager Art Ross sold star goaltender Tiny Thompson to Detroit. Thompson, a ten-year veteran, had won four Vezina Trophies and was extremely popular throughout New England. But Ross already had a replacement for Thompson in mind, a young goalie from Minnesota named Frank Brimsek, who had been playing for Providence in the American League.

If Brimsek was nervous about taking over for a legend, he didn't show it. In fact, he made the most sensational goaltending debut in NHL history.

In his first game against Montreal, Brimsek was unflappable and made a dozen brilliant saves. Still, he and the Bruins lost the game 2–0. In his next seven starts, Brimsek embarked on a streak that astonished the world of hockey. It began with a 4–0 shutout of the Blackhawks in Chicago. Two nights later, he blanked Chicago again by a 2–0 score. He followed up with a 3–0 shutout over the New York Rangers. Three shutouts in a row!

In his fifth NHL game, the rookie helped the Bruins edge the Montreal Canadiens 3–2. In his next three games, he didn't allow a goal, blanking the Canadiens 1–0, the Detroit Red Wings 2–0, and the New York Americans 2–0. The rookie had compiled six shutouts in his first eight games. When asked about his brilliant start, Brimsek kidded, "Well, I knew I had to get off to a fast start. I knew darn well if I had a slow start I might be on the next train back to Providence."

By then Boston fans had picked out a suitable nickname for their new goalie – Mr. Zero. Brimsek went on to win the Calder Trophy that season (with ten shutouts and a 1.59 goals-against average). He also captured the Vezina Trophy, gained a berth on the All Star team, and saw his name engraved on the 1939 Stanley Cup, when the Bruins eliminated the Toronto Maple Leafs four games to one in the finals. All in all, a spectacular rookie season – one for the record books.

Goalie Hall's Streak Will Last Forever

No matter how impressive they appear, records, streaks, and other great accomplishments are often surpassed by others. That's the nature of the game. But one record/streak/ accomplishment that is bound to occupy a page in the NHL record book forever is held by former NHL goalie Glenn Hall.

When Glenn Hall entered his teens, he was captain of his minor hockey team in Humboldt, Saskatchewan. But one night, none of his teammates would agree to play in goal. So Hall shrugged and agreed to play in goal himself. In time, he became a star, playing the position so brilliantly that he became a famous big leaguer with Detroit, Chicago, and St. Louis. In retirement, he became an honored member of the Hockey Hall of Fame.

In the late 1950s and early '60s, no NHL team relied more on its goaltender than the Chicago Blackhawks. During those years, Glenn Hall was always ready – if not eager – to play in every game. The games and seasons piled up and goaltender endurance records began to fall. Hall performed in 300 consecutive games, then 400 consecutive games, then 500 consecutive games. Hall established a record for durability that may last forever. He played in every regular season game for more than seven NHL seasons. When his back pain became so severe that he couldn't bend over, he was forced to leave a game on November 7, 1962. By then, he had played in 502 consecutive games, or more than 33,000 minutes. Hall's record is assured because of the two-goalie system. It has been more than twenty-five years since an NHL goalie, Eddie Johnston of Boston, played in all of his team's games in a season.

Hall established the record despite many injuries and nervous tension so severe that it caused him to throw up before games and between periods. Many times he confessed he hated tending goal. The fact that he won the Calder Trophy and captured three Vezina Trophies and a Stanley Cup helped make up for the agony he felt every time he had to face the best shooters in the NHL.

Women Goalies Make History

During the 1993–94 hockey season, three women goalies were invited to display their talent in men's hockey at the professional level.

On October 30, Erin Whitten, a twenty-two-year old netminder from Glens Falls, New York, became the first woman to be credited with a goaltending victory in one of the minor pro leagues, the East Coast Hockey League. Whitten led the Toledo Storm to a 6–5 victory over the Dayton Bombers. The former New Hampshire University star won her second game two days later. Even though she gave up ten goals, her teammates scored eleven. It is unlikely any other goalie, male or female, in any pro league, skated off with a win after allowing goals that reached double figures.

Just one week later, twenty-one-year-old Manon Rheaume, playing for Knoxville in the same league, became the second female goalie to win a game in pro hockey. Later she would move to Nashville in the East Coast Hockey League and win five of six starts.

Before the season was over, a third female goalie won a game, this time in Florida's Sunshine Hockey League. Kelly Dyer, twenty-seven, who was current NHL goalie Tom Barrasso's backup goalie in high school, led her team, the West Palm Beach Blaze, to a 6–2 victory over the Daytona Beach Sun Devils.

The Reluctant Goaltender

Have you heard the story of the aging NHL coach who was forced to play in goal for his team during the Stanley Cup play-offs? It happened in Montreal in 1928, in a final series between the Montreal Maroons and the New York Rangers.

After losing the series opener, the Rangers ran into real trouble in game two. Star goaltender Lorne Chabot was knocked flat by a Nels Stewart shot and left the ice with blood streaming from a cut over his eye. In those days, teams carried just one goaltender, and with no spare goaltender on his bench, coach Lester Patrick was handed an edict – find a substitute goalie in ten minutes or forfeit the game. His players provided the solution. "Coach, why don't you go in the net? We'll play extra hard if we know you're in goal."

So white-haired Lester Patrick, age forty-four, decided to don the pads himself. If the Maroons felt that Patrick would be an easy mark when they saw him shuffle awkwardly onto the ice, they were mistaken. Patrick played remarkably well, allowing just one goal in eighteen shots. Patrick's Rangers won the game in overtime. In the dressing room, Patrick played down his performance.

"Heck, I stopped only half a dozen hard shots," he said. "My players saved the old man with their backchecking."

The Rangers, with Joe Miller taking over in goal, went on to win the Stanley Cup that spring, and they were treated like heroes when they returned to New York. Especially Lester Patrick, the coach-turned-goaltender.

About Those Oldtime Goalies

In old hockey photos you often see goaltenders wearing caps on their heads. Some wore them to keep warm. Others to provide a little protection, not from the players on the ice, but from the fans. In early-day hockey, fans often threw things at the netminders. Some would even bring peashooters to the game and use the goalie as a target.

Early day goaltenders wore ordinary shin pads. In 1896, Whitey Merritt, a Winnipeg goalie, showed up in a Stanley Cup series wearing white cricket pads to protect his shins, and the idea was quickly copied by all goalies.

Goalies, then as now, were often temperamental. One early-day goalie, Fred Chittick of Ottawa, refused to suit up for his team when management wouldn't give him a number of complimentary tickets to home games. Another goalie raced down the ice with the puck and scored a goal.

Goalie Percy Lesueur used the same goal stick in all league and play-off games for five consecutive seasons. The stick is on display at the Hockey Hall of Fame in Toronto.

Thank Plante – and a Woman – for Goalie Face Masks

Hall of Fame goalie Jacques Plante wasn't the first NHL goalie to wear a face mask, but he deserves most of the credit for making the mask a vital piece of goaltending equipment.

Plante, star goalie with the Montreal Canadiens for many years, first wore a home-made mask he invented in 1959 after suffering a gash on his nose during a game in New York. Many years earlier, in 1930, goalie Clint Benedict of the Ottawa Senators stopped a Howie Morenz shot with his nose and immediately asked a Boston manu-facturer to create a mask. The mask, made of leather, covered the nose but made it difficult to see pucks at the goalie's feet. So Benedict discarded it and then retired from hockey.

But a little-known woman goalie from Queen's University can justly claim to be the first hockey player to wear a face mask. In 1927 Elizabeth Graham, playing for the university women's team, wore a fencing mask during the hockey season. Graham's innovation did not begin a trend. In fact, her novel idea earned her a small paragraph in a Montreal newspaper and nothing more.

CHAPTER 9

DARING DEFENSE

Highest Scoring Defensemen Both Wore 77

Raymond Bourque enjoyed the rare honor of having his jersey Number 77 retired by two NHL clubs – the Boston Bruins and the Colorado Avalanche.

After more than twenty seasons as the best Bruins defenseman since Bobby Orr, Bourque requested a trade to a Stanley Cup contender. His request was granted and a few months later he led the Colorado Avalanche to the 2001 Stanley Cup. Bourque retired a few days later, holding several impressive records. He's the only defenseman to score more than 400 goals (410) and the only one to collect 1579 points. He won five Norris Trophies as the NHL's top defenseman and he was runner-up for the award five times. He's the only player in history to make nineteen consecutive All Star appearances. He also played more games without winning the Stanley Cup than any other player. It's something he just laughs about, now that he has lifted the trophy in triumph.

When the Avalanche retired Bourque's Number 77 in November 2001, each one of the Avalanche players wore jersey Number 77 in the warm up before a game with Edmonton. All twenty-two jerseys were then signed by Bourque and auctioned off during the game. A minimum bid of $500 was required for each jersey, and the highest bidder was rewarded with a trip for two to accompany the team on a road trip. Incredibly, three of the bids were for $30,000. The auction raised $186,000 for the New York Police and Fire Widows Benefit Fund, and the Colorado organization agreed to take all three bidders on the road trip to Minnesota.

Bourque was pushed hard for the title of hockey's highest scoring defenseman by another Number 77 – Paul Coffey. Coffey, who played for twenty-one seasons with nine different teams, wound up with 396 goals, only fourteen less than Bourque. Coffey was a three-time winner of the Norris Trophy and was a member of four Stanley Cup teams, three with Edmonton and one with Pittsburgh. Here's a statistical comparison of the two great defensemen:

	Years	Games	Goals	Assists	Points
Bourque	22	1612	410	1169	1579
Coffey	21	1409	396	1135	1531

What a close race it was between these future Hall of Famers! They finished far ahead of all other high-scoring defensemen, including Bobby Orr, Brad Park, Denis Potvin, and Chris Chelios.

It's just a coincidence that Ray Bourque and Paul Coffey both wore jerseys with the number 77. When Coffey was picked up by Boston in 2000 – his ninth team in a twenty-one-year career – he found that Number 77 was unavailable. It had been retired in honor of Bourque's great career as a Bruin. Coffey shrugged and settled for Number 74.

Bobby Orr Shoots to the Top

From the 1966–67 season – the year before the NHL expanded from six teams to twelve – until 1978–79, Bobby Orr was the most exciting player in hockey.

Before Orr arrived in the NHL, hockey people thought it impossible for a defenseman to win the Art Ross Trophy, awarded annually to the highest scorer in the game. It didn't take Orr long to change their thinking. In his first season as a Boston Bruin, he set a goal scoring record for defenseman with 21 goals. In 1969–70, he amazed everyone by finishing on top of the NHL scoring race with 120 points, twenty-one more than team-mate Phil Esposito. Before Orr, no defenseman had ever come close to winning a scoring title. It was unthinkable. To prove it was no fluke, Orr topped all scorers again five years later, this time with 135 points. In between he finished second three times and third once (all four times behind Esposito).

What made Bobby Orr's accomplishments even more remarkable was that he played for most of his career on knees so badly injured he often wondered how they held him up. He would no sooner have one knee operation when he'd start planning for the next one. In all, he thinks he had thirteen or fourteen operations on his knees, some after he retired from the game.

While Orr's scarred knees and his scoring titles have been well-publicized, one of his most amazing records has not been – his career plus-minus rating. For his 657-game career, Bobby was a plus 597. That means he was on the ice for 1188 even-strength goals by his team and on the ice for only 591 goals against his team. No wonder Don Cherry, who coached him in Boston, refers to Orr as, "the greatest player in hockey history."

Bobby Baun's Most Famous Goal

Bobby Baun was not a goal scorer. As a rugged defenseman, he wasn't expected to be. In ninety-six play-off games Baun scored only three times. But one of those three goals was by far his biggest. It came against the Detroit Red Wings in the 1964 Stanley Cup finals, and it's still talked about to this day. Baun has even written a book in which he devotes full attention to that goal.

With the Toronto Maple Leafs in 1964, Baun was a fearless defender who stepped in front of a Gordie Howe shot during the sixth game of a wildly exciting final play-off series. Detroit could clinch with a victory; the Leafs needed two more wins.

At stake that night was the Stanley Cup and, with time running out, the score was tied. Baun crumpled in a heap after Howe's shot struck his ankle and he was carried off the ice on a stretcher. The Red Wings medics examined Baun's leg and suggested he take the rest of the night off. Baun said, "Can you freeze my ankle?" Out came the needle.

Baun hobbled back on the ice and, early in the first overtime frame, the puck came to him at the point inside the Red Wings zone. He shot wildly toward Terry Sawchuk, the Detroit goalie. He didn't expect to score, but the puck flew at defenseman Bill Gadsby, caromed off his stick, and bounded into the net behind Sawchuk. Baun's looping shot won the game for the Leafs and forced a seventh game in the series. Two days later, back at Maple Leaf Gardens, the Leafs blanked the Red Wings 4–0 and captured the Stanley

Cup. Only then did Baun, who played in the final game, consent to have x-rays taken of his damaged ankle. Sure enough, the bone was cracked. Baun's broken-ankle goal has become a hockey legend.

Picard Visits the Wrong Bench

When the St. Louis Blues joined the NHL in 1967–68, one of their most popular players was Noel Picard, a towering defenseman from Quebec. Despite his eagerness to contribute to his team's success, there were occasions when Picard didn't appear to be totally focused on the game.

Midway through an important game against the Boston Bruins, Picard finished his shift, called for someone to replace him, and headed toward his team's bench. But somehow he lost his way. He never could explain why, but he wound up at the Bruins bench by mistake.

The Boston trainer saw Picard approaching, and he threw the gate open and waved him in. Stifling their laughter, the Bruins shifted along the bench to make room for Picard. Picard caught his breath and play resumed. Only then did he notice that everyone around him was dressed in Boston colors. "Can you believe this?" he asked the nearest Bruin. "What am I going to do now?"

By then everyone was laughing at his predicament, everyone but Blues coach Scotty Bowman, whose glare made Picard squirm with embarrassment. The big defenseman decided to act. When the puck was chased into the Bruins zone, he bolted over the boards, dashed across the ice, and dove in among his teammates. "I was praying nobody would notice me," he explained later.

But the keen-eyed referee had spotted Picard's leap off the Bruins bench and blew his whistle. "Too many men on the ice!" he barked, penalizing the Blues and causing Scotty Bowman's blood pressure to soar even higher.

Picard could only hang his head. He knew his gaffe would provide laughs for years to come. And whenever it did, he laughed about it too.

Brewer's Cute Trick

Carl Brewer was a talented defenseman for the Toronto Maple Leafs. Brewer impressed everybody with the way he would deal with opponents who dared to stand in front of the Leafs net. Referee Vern Buffey in particular marveled at the way Brewer played his position, throwing bigger men off balance and making them look like incompetent bumblers whenever they tried to outmuscle Brewer.

One night there was a brawl, and gloves and sticks littered the ice. When Buffey and his linesmen restored order, Buffey noticed an unusual-looking hockey glove lying on the ice. The ref examined it, and found the glove had no palm. Why would a player cut the palms out of his gloves? When Carl Brewer claimed the glove, Buffey had his answer.

In goal-mouth skirmishes, Brewer had been slipping his hands through the holes in his gloves and grabbing opponents by their jerseys. A good grip meant he was able to toss them backwards, forwards, or sideways and throw them off balance. Buffey's discovery of Brewer's cute trick led to a new NHL rule – no more palmless hockey gloves.

Brewer went on to contribute much more to hockey than a rules change. In 1994, he organized a group of former players who charged the NHL with skimming surplus money from their pension fund. An Ontario court agreed, and the NHL was required to pay an estimated $40 million, which was distributed to retired players. Those ex-players will be forever grateful to Brewer, who passed away from a heart attack in September 2001.

CHAPTER 10
FANTASTIC FORWARDS

"I'll Score Fifty," the Rookie Promised

Prior to the 1977 NHL entry draft, New York Islanders scout Henry Saraceno took manager Bill Torrey aside and said, "Bill, you've got to take Mike Bossy in the draft. He's going to be in the Hall of Fame someday. I'm sure of it."

Torrey had heard some negative things about young Bossy. "For one thing, he was a skinny kid," Torrey would later say. "Not much muscle and prone to injuries. What's more, his defensive play was not up to NHL standards and he hated fighting."

But there was no question the kid could score. In Pee Wee hockey, Bossy had made headlines by scoring fifteen goals in one period of hockey. In his junior career, the slim right winger had tallied 309 career goals – only five fewer than the record held by Guy Lafleur.

"You may be right, Henry," Torrey responded. "But it's a tough decision. Besides, Bossy may not be around when the Islanders get to draft – we're number fifteen on the list."

On draft day, fourteen juniors were selected – among them six right wingers – and Bossy's name had not been called. Obviously, the other general managers, like Torrey, were concerned about Bossy's passive nature and his defensive play. Torrey took a deep breath, made up his mind, and claimed Bossy for the Islanders. "I'm sure it was the happiest day of Henry's life," Torrey would say at Saraceno's funeral two years later.

At his first training camp, Bossy displayed loads of confidence. When Torrey asked the rookie how many goals he planned to score as a rookie, Bossy brashly replied, "Oh, I should get fifty."

And he did. In 1977–78, he pumped home twenty goals in his first twenty-two games, and went on to establish a rookie record for goals with 53, erasing the previous record of 44 set by Buffalo's Richard Martin.

Fifty-goal seasons became Bossy's trademark. In nine seasons as an Islander he never scored less than fifty, a feat no other player – not even Wayne Gretzky – had achieved. And he would have scored fifty in his tenth season if a back injury hadn't cramped his style and forced him into early retirement.

For Bossy's nine seasons, no one was happier to have him around than Torrey. "I'm so proud of Michael and his accomplishments. All the records he set, the Calder Trophy, the All Star teams, the four Stanley Cups, 573 goals, and the Hall of Fame – just like Henry Saraceno predicted. I just wish he'd lived to see it."

Bossy's rookie record of 53 goals lasted until 1992–93, when Teemu Selanne of the Winnipeg Jets established a new mark of 76. But fifty goals or more for nine consecutive years? That record should stand for a long time.

McGee a Turn-of-the-Century Gretzky

At the turn of the 20th century, a young Ottawa scoring star named Frank McGee gained fame as one of the finest hockey players in the world. To his legion of fans, he was the greatest stickhandler ever to carry a puck down the ice. But there were others who said he shouldn't even be on the ice, for he played with a disability.

McGee was the star of the fabled Ottawa Silver Seven, Stanley Cup champions. One night, early in his career, an opposing player smashed into McGee and knocked him unconscious. McGee was carried off, bleeding from deep cut over his eye. Surgeons tried to save the eye but the damage was too severe – McGee was permanently blinded in one eye. From then on he was known as One-Eyed Frank McGee. Despite the urging of his friends to give up the game, McGee returned to hockey.

In the years that followed, McGee set some amazing records. In a 1905 Stanley Cup game against Dawson City, he scored 14 goals, a mark no player has ever tied or topped. In one play-off match, wearing tape to protect a broken wrist, he scored the tying and winning goals for Ottawa in a Cup-clinching game – he wore tape around both wrists that night to confuse opposing players. During his career, McGee scored 71 goals in twenty-three regular-season games, and another 63 goals in twenty-two play-off matches. No player, before or since, has averaged almost three goals per game.

McGee was a gentlemanly player who was idolized for his stylish play and his good looks. His white hockey pants were always freshly laundered and creased with an iron, and his blond hair was always combed neatly to one side. He was a born leader, and when World War I broke out, he was anxious to serve. Despite his handicap, he was able to join the Canadian infantry by having a friend enlist in his name. He quickly rose from a private to a captain's rank. Overseas, during the winter of 1916, in the middle of a fierce battle in France, an enemy shell ended the life of Frank McGee, one of hockey's greatest heroes. Hockey fans everywhere mourned the loss of this fine sportsman.

First Black Player Was Willie O'Ree

Willie O'Ree, the first black player to perform on an NHL team, was a swift-skating left winger from Fredericton, New Brunswick. His first stint with the Boston Bruins, in January 1958, was barely mentioned by the media – a mere two games against the Montreal Canadiens. He recalls, "We beat the Habs at the Forum 3–0 and, back in Boston the following night, they beat us 5–3. That was it. I was told my two-game trial was over. By Monday I was back in the minors. I waited four and a half years before Boston called me up again." This time he stayed around for forty-three games.

What the Bruins didn't know was that O'Ree was playing with a handicap. Years earlier, playing for the Kitchener-Waterloo Canucks in junior hockey, he had been struck in the face by a puck and lost 95 percent vision in one eye. But he refused to give up the game. He turned pro in 1956–57 with the Quebec Aces, a minor league team, signing for $3500. He neglected to tell his employers that he was legally blind, fearing he would be barred from playing if he did.

In the NHL, he heard a lot of racial slurs. "But never in Boston," he says. "My teammates supported me there. They accepted me totally. All of them had class."

How much did the first black player in the NHL earn? "I recall signing with the

Bruins for $3500," he says. "That was precisely my minor league salary. It may not sound like much but I was thrilled to get it."

And his best memory of the big league? "That's easy," he says. "I scored the winning goal against the Canadiens on January 1, 1961 – New Year's Day. I'll never forget the reception I got from the Boston fans when that puck went in. The ovation lasted for more than two minutes."

It was a well-earned salute to the first black player to score a goal in the NHL. In 1998, the NHL honored O'Ree for his pioneering efforts and named him director of youth hockey development for the NHL/U.S.A. Hockey Diversity Task Force. He now travels all over North America teaching kids hockey skills and life skills.

Pat Verbeek's Lucky Day

For the past two decades, Pat Verbeek has been one of hockey's best right wingers. He has also been one of the luckiest players in the game because, at one time, it appeared that his career might be over because of a careless off-season accident. In the spring of 1985, while working on his 200-acre farm near Forest, Ontario, Verbeek's left thumb was completely severed when he caught his hand in a corn-planting machine.

The thumb dropped into a load of fertilizer, and while Pat was rushed to a hospital in nearby Sarnia, his parents searched frantically for the thumb. One of them finally located it and drove at breakneck speed to the hospital where it was re-attached. But the surgeon didn't offer Verbeek much hope that the operation would be a success. "Pat, you may never play hockey again," he said. "A player can't grip his stick without a healthy thumb."

But soon, circulation returned to the thumb. Verbeek began lifting weights and squeezing grips to strengthen his hand. And he predicted he would be back playing when the new season got underway. "I think the thumb has even grown a bit," he quipped at training camp. "Because of all that fertilizer it fell in."

Pat made an amazing recovery. He came back to score twenty-five goals that year. And fifteen years later he was still scoring goals at a Hall of Fame pace. In 2000–01, as a member of the Dallas Stars, he joined twenty-seven other NHLers in the 500-goal club.

Barber's Dentures Disappeared

There was a mystery to be solved during the 1981 All Star game played in Los Angeles. Winger Bill Barber of the Philadelphia Flyers, who had slipped his dentures into a paper cup in the dressing room before the game, came back during the first intermission to find them missing. *Who would steal my teeth*, he thought? *I can't go back to Philadelphia without them.*

Part of the riddle was solved when arena maintenance employees admitted they had entered the team dressing rooms with brooms and dustpans while the first period was underway. They swept up everything in sight, including every paper cup.

At first Barber thought it was a practical joke. He had heard that a Montreal player, while the Habs were on a road trip, had gathered up his teammates' dentures from similar paper cups and mailed them back to the Montreal Forum. And Toronto captain George Armstrong once switched goalie Johnny Bower's dentures with a similar-looking set, claiming later that he had picked them up from an undertaker friend. But this was no joke. Barber's teeth had simply vanished.

The arena workers spent the second period sorting through a ton of garbage and looking into a thousand paper cups. Still no choppers. The search went on, and finally a worker pawing through a garbage can flipped over a paper cup, looked inside, and smiled. Smiling back at him were Barber's false teeth.

The discovery came just in time, for Barber had played so well he was to be interviewed on television after the game. And photographers were snapping his picture. When they said, "Smile, Bill," he was happy to oblige.

A Most Embarrassing Moment

Jackie Hamilton was a young center who broke in with the Toronto Maple Leafs in 1942 at the tender age of sixteen. Jackie defies any other NHLer to match his most embarrassing moment in hockey.

"I took a shot on goal one night just as a big defenseman caught me with a hip check. He sent me flying high in the air and I figured I was going to go into orbit. Then my

skate lodged in the wire netting behind the goal – there was no glass in those days – and I was stuck up there. So there I am, turned upside down with my head about two feet off the ice. And I stayed that way for the longest time. The boys kept on playing. I was hollerin' for somebody to come and rescue me. Meanwhile, the rival goalie kept lookin' back over his shoulder to tell me what a dirty so-and-so I was, and the fans of course thought it was hilarious. Finally, I heard a whistle and my teammates came over and helped to get me down. I'll bet I'm the only NHL player who ever suffered through an experience like that."

Jackie Hamilton revealed his best-kept hockey secret. "Sometimes, if there was a key face-off to be won, I'd go to the bench and take a swig of water which I'd hold in my mouth. Just as the puck was dropped, I'd spray the opposing center with the water – right in the face. It always took him by surprise and distracted him. The referee caught me at it one night and gave me a penalty. But he didn't know what to call it. I think he called it two minutes for spraying!"

Sneaks In, Scores the Winner

In October 1967, forward Bill Sutherland was forced to sneak into the home opener of the Philadelphia Flyers. It was the night the Flyers made their NHL debut, and Sutherland hoped to play well in his first game for his new team.

What a surprise he received when he arrived at the rink! Nobody knew him and nobody would let him in.

"But I'm playing tonight," he protested. "I'm one of the Flyers."

"Prove it," snapped the man attending the gate.

When Sutherland couldn't produce anything to show he was on the Flyer payroll, he was told to buy a ticket. "Nobody gets in without a ticket," he was told.

When the attendant turned his back to look after some paying fans, Sutherland saw his opportunity. He dashed through the turnstiles and ran down the corridor to the safety of the Philadelphia dressing room while the ticket taker yelled, "Stop that man!" An hour later, when he skated out to face the Pittsburgh Penguins, he vowed to do something that would catch the attention of the rink attendants, so they would always recognize him. Early in the third period he scored the only goal of the game to give the Flyers a 1–0 victory.

This Gamble Paid Off

The Philadelphia Flyers gambled and won in 1969 when they drafted center Bobby Clarke, a two-time Western Canada Hockey League scoring champion from Flin Flon, Manitoba. All the other NHL clubs had scouted Clarke and liked his style, but they were aware he suffered from diabetes and was therefore considered to be a high-risk choice.

Despite his disease, which required daily injections of insulin, Clarke was coveted by the Philadelphia Flyers, who were more than willing to gamble on him. Clarke became the seventeenth player selected in the draft. Looking back, it turned out to be one of the best moves the Flyers ever made. None of the players drafted ahead of Clarke enjoyed the Hall of Fame career he did.

Clarke quickly became the heart and soul of the Flyers franchise, winning three Hart Trophies as the league's Most Valuable Player and leading Philadelphia to back-to-back Stanley Cups in 1974 and '75. And he'll long be remembered for his gritty play on a line with Ron Ellis and Paul Henderson in Team Canada's dramatic win over the Soviet Union during the first great international series in 1972. In 1987, Clarke's jersey Number 16 was retired and he was inducted into the Hockey Hall of Fame. He continues to serve the Flyers as general manager and team president.

Wings Create Highest Scoring Line in History

When coach Scotty Bowman of the Detroit Red Wings placed veteran wingers Brett Hull and Luc Robitaille on a line with team captain and center Steve Yzerman at the start of the 2000–01 season, he created a threesome with the most career goals in NHL history.

Hull, an off-season free agent, joined the Wings with 657 career goals, sixth on the all-time scoring list. Robitaille, another free agent, was twelfth on the list with 602 goals. Yzerman, eighth on the list with 651 goals, is the longest-serving captain in the NHL, with sixteen years of service wearing the "C" for Detroit. All three would like to surpass 700 goals before they retire.

NHL defensemen and goaltenders might be a little nervous facing a line that has collectively scored more than 2000 goals.

Flying Finn Highest Scoring European

Can you name the former NHL star who was inducted into the Hockey Hall of Fame in 2001 as the highest scoring European player ever to perform in the NHL? Here's a hint. He was a key figure in five Stanley Cup victories by the Edmonton Oilers in the 1980s. As an Oiler, he was always overshadowed by a man named Gretzky. But Gretzky is the first to admit, "If it hadn't been for my linemate from Finland, I'd never have scored as many goals or points as I did. He was the perfect winger."

His name, of course, is Jari Kurri. He scored fifty or more goals in a season four times, and finished his career with a total of 601 goals. In 1984–85, he set an NHL mark for right wingers with 71 goals, joining Wayne Gretzky and Phil Esposito as the third NHL scorer to top seventy. He's not only the highest scoring player from Europe, but he shares the NHL record (with Reg Leach) for most play-off goals in a season with 19.

In his native Finland, Kurri is idolized by young players, in the same manner Gretzky and Lemieux are revered in North America. And why shouldn't he be? He's earned his place in hockey as one of the greatest scorers to play the game.

CHAPTER 11

GREAT ONES

Fetisov Best European Player

Moscow-born Viacheslav Fetisov has been voted by *The Hockey News* as the best European player of all time. Fetisov was a brilliant player at the tender age of eighteen when he joined the Red Army team in the Soviet Elite League. For the next two decades he maintained a level of play equal to most of the best NHL defensemen. Fetisov and teammate Igor Larionov are the only two players to win Olympic gold medals, World Championship gold medals, a Canada Cup title, a World Junior Championship gold medal – and two Stanley Cups. On three occasions Fetisov was named the top player in Europe.

In 1978 the Montreal Canadiens drafted him; he was their first-ever European selection. But the Habs let his name slide from their list and the New Jersey Devils jumped in and claimed him in the 1983 draft. It took until 1989 for him to get a visa to allow him to live in the U.S. and join the Devils, a team that counted heavily on his leadership for the next five and a half years. Even then, well into his thirties, he was a standout on defense. Wayne Gretzky called him "the hardest man in the league to beat one-on-one."

During the 1995–96 season he was traded to Detroit, where he joined other Russian stars and helped the Red Wings capture a pair of Stanley Cups.

After a party for the second Cup victory in 1998, Fetisov was in a limousine that crashed into a tree. In the accident, his good friend Vladimir Konstantinov suffered brain damage that ended his career. According to *The Hockey News*, Fetisov suffered nerve damage in the accident, kept quiet about it, and played the following season with almost no feeling in one leg. But by then, after twenty-two years of world-class hockey, it was time to retire.

Recently, Fetisov became only the second Soviet player (after goaltender Vladislav Tretiak) to be inducted into the Hockey Hall of Fame. In 2002, Fetisov coached the Russian team to a bronze medal at the Salt Lake City Olympics.

Dominik Dominates

For five seasons in the 1980s, Dominik Hasek was named Czechoslovakian Goaltender-of-the-Year. For three of those seasons he was named his country's Player-of-the-Year. It couldn't get much better than that for Dominik – at least in his homeland, so that's where he chose to play.

The Chicago Blackhawks showed some interest in the Czech star when he was still a teenager, selecting him in the 1983 entry draft in the eleventh round. But several seasons would go by before Hasek showed up in Chicago. By then, in 1990–91, the Hawks had an outstanding goaltender in Ed Belfour and Hasek played in only five games, winning three. The following season he won ten of twenty starts and was named to the NHL All-Rookie team, even though he had spent half the season in the minors. At age twenty-seven, the rookie realized the years were slipping by and he still hadn't proven, to himself or anyone else, that he was one of the world's great netminders.

His opportunity would come, not in Chicago, but in Buffalo. A midsummer trade in 1992 sent him to the Sabres. In his second season in Buffalo, his career took off. He wound up with a 1.95 goals-against average, becoming the first goalie to record a goals-against average of under 2.00 since Bernie Parent's 1.89 in 1973–74. He captured the Vezina Trophy and a First Team All Star berth in five of the next six seasons. He won back-to-back Hart Trophies as NHL MVP – the first goalie to do so. The last goaltender to win the Hart had been Jacques Plante in 1962.

When *The Hockey News* listed the players who had helped create the forty greatest NHL seasons, Hasek was named twice by a panel of experts, for his 1993–94 and 1997–98 seasons. In 1998 he led his Czech teammates to an Olympic gold medal at Nagano, Japan, beating Russia 1–0 in the finals. He failed to repeat as a medal winner in the 2002 Olympics at Salt Lake City. But 2002 did see Hasek, with the Detroit Red Wings for his final NHL season, achieve the honor he cherishes most – the name Hasek engraved on the Stanley Cup.

More about Orr

When Bobby Orr signed a contract to play for the Boston Bruins in 1966–67, for a reported salary of $60,000 over two years, he became the highest paid rookie in NHL history. He went on from there to become one of the greatest players in the game.

"He was the greatest," says Don Cherry, his former coach. In 1997, *The Hockey News* conducted a survey, attempting to discover who was the better player, Orr or Wayne Gretzky. Gretzky, who played eight more seasons than Orr, was the choice of voters by a narrow margin. The difference was less than 1 percent. In 2000, *The Hockey News* conducted another vote. A panel of experts was asked to name the most significant full-season performance by an NHL player. This time Orr edged Gretzky by the slimmest of margins – 864 votes to 857. Orr's 1969–70 season, in which he became the first defenseman to win the scoring title with 120 points, was seen as the most significant full season by an NHL player. Gretzky's 92-goal, 212-point season in 1981–82 received just seven fewer votes in the balloting.

Before knee injuries forced Orr to retire at age thirty, he had almost single-handedly brought the Bruins from last place to first. He helped them to two Stanley Cups and he smashed most scoring records for defensemen. During the 1969–70 season, he won four major trophies: the Hart (regular-season Most Valuable Player), the Norris (best defenseman), the Art Ross (scoring leader), and the Conn Smythe (play-off MVP).

No other player has ever earned so much silverware in one NHL season. And no wonder the Bruins fans were so eager to honor him on a January night in 1979. They had let him slip away to Chicago for a couple of seasons. Everyone knew it was a mistake, a move engineered by his agent, the notorious Al Eagleson. Now he was back on Boston ice, where he belonged, watching his famous Number 4 being raised to the rafters at the Boston Garden. His fans roared their approval during an ovation that lasted ten minutes, fifteen minutes . . . twenty-five minutes. Never before and not since has there been such a deafening tribute to a beloved Boston athlete.

Mario the Magician

When Pittsburgh's great star Mario Lemieux first retired after the 1996–97 season following a battle with cancer and two major back surgeries, he had captured the league scoring crown six times, helped win two Stanley Cups, and scored 613 career goals. His goals-per-game average of .823 was the highest in history, higher even than Wayne Gretzky's. And his points-per-game average of 2.005 was also the highest in history. As one opposing goalie said, "Mario's a magician with the puck."

But there were times he played in great pain. "With all my health problems and injuries, I realized how fragile life can be," said Mario. "And how fortunate I was to be a hockey player and win two Stanley Cups. But there were so many people less fortunate." Mario formed the Mario Lemieux Foundation to raise money and make grants to families of cancer victims.

When Mario's health showed dramatic improvement, he returned to the NHL in spectacular fashion in the 2000–01 season – scoring 35 goals and 76 points in forty-three games. *The Hockey News* called his comeback unbelievable.

He also returned with a much greater responsibility to his team. On June 24, 1999, Lemieux became the first player-turned-owner in major pro sports after pledging $20 million to keep the Penguins afloat and in Pittsburgh. Deciding to become an owner wasn't a difficult decision for Mario. The team owed him $32.5 million. What better way to collect it than to own the club?

A one-of-a-kind feat in the 1988–89 season sets Mario apart from other great scorers. He scored five goals in a game and each one was scored in a different manner – an even-strength goal, a short-handed goal, a power-play goal, a penalty-shot goal, and an empty-net goal – in an 8–6 win over New Jersey. Mario also picked up three assists in the game.

As he grows older, Mario's ability to maintain his points-per-game average matters less and less. He saved the Penguins and hockey is richer for having him back on the ice. Canadians are particularly proud of Mario for the leadership qualities he showed in helping Canada win a gold medal in the 2002 Olympic Games. Mario is the only active NHL player entitled to wear a Hockey Hall of Fame jacket and ring. He was inducted in 1997.

Two Superstars Excel in the '87 Canada Cup

The 1987 Canada Cup – featuring a three-game final for the first time in history – produced another classic confrontation between the best of the Soviets and the best players in the NHL. It also made teammates of two of hockey's greatest players, Wayne Gretzky and Mario Lemieux.

In the best-of-three final series, played in Hamilton, Ontario, the Soviets took game one 6–5. Then, in game two, Mario Lemieux scored three times as Team Canada won in double overtime 6–5.

The final game was one of the most exciting games ever played. Team Canada coach Mike Keenan played Gretzky and Lemieux on the same line in this crucial match – and they clicked immediately. They played marvelous hockey together in a thrilling 6–5 victory. Gretzky collected five assists and Lemieux came through with his second straight hat trick.

One of the most exciting goals ever seen in hockey was Lemieux's second straight game winner. But this one didn't require overtime. The score was tied at 5 late in the game. Lemieux took a pass from Gretzky, who had carried it deep into the Soviet zone, and blasted a shot past goalie Sergei Mylnikov. It was Lemieux's eleventh goal of the series – a tournament record – and it came with 1:24 remaining on the clock. Team Canada had captured another Canada Cup!

The tournament was credited with making a complete player of Mario Lemieux. In that tournament he proved his greatness once and for all. He said, "Scoring the game-winning goal in that final game was my greatest thrill ever." Now that moment will be relegated to second place on his list of great thrills. Winning an Olympic gold medal in hockey tops everything.

Gretzky's Stats Are Amazing

It sounds impossible, but if Wayne Gretzky had never scored a goal during his NHL career, he would still reign as the all-time scoring champion. The Great One would be the leader on his number of assists alone. In twenty seasons with four different clubs, Gretzky collected 894 goals, 1963 assists, and 2857 points. In twenty-six seasons, Gordie Howe, who holds second place on the all-time scoring list, scored 801 goals, and added

1049 assists for 1850 points. You can see that Howe's total points, tallied over six more seasons than Gretzky, still don't add up to Wayne's assist total.

Many of Gretzky's records may last well into the current century. Among today's players, can you name anyone who is likely to equal or surpass the following marks?

Most goals, one season	92
Most goals, one season, including play-offs	100
Most goals, fifty games from start of season	61 (twice)
Most assists, one season	163
Most assists, one season, including play-offs	174
Most points, one season	215
Most points, one season, including play-offs	255
Most three-or-more-goal games, career	50
Longest consecutive point scoring streak	51 games

Gretzky is the only player to score five goals in a game on four occasions. He's the only player to win ten Art Ross Trophies as NHL scoring champion and eight Hart Trophies as MVP. People often say records are made to be broken. But some of Wayne's appear to be insurmountable.

Little Known Facts about the Great One

Wayne Gretzky's astonishing exploits in professional hockey have been well documented, like his 92 goals and 212 points as an Edmonton Oiler in 1981–82. He continued to excel after he retired as a player, by directing Team Canada to a gold medal triumph in the 2002 Olympics, Canada's first such medal in fifty years. But some of the records he set as a pint-sized player in minor hockey are just as amazing as anything he accomplished as a professional.

Gretzky's first season in organized hockey was rather ordinary. Playing against older boys he scored just one goal. Two seasons later, as a nine-year-old, he scored 196 goals and 120 assists. His exceptional feats began to be noticed by the media. By the time he reached the Pee Wee level, he was phenomenal. He scored an incredible 378 goals in one eighty-two-game season.

In one game, Gretzky's team was trailing 8–0. He sparked an amazing third-period comeback and his team came out ahead 11–10.

In one tournament, he scored 50 goals in nine games, and by the time he was thirteen he had already reached an unheard-of plateau – 1000 career goals. At the Quebec City Pee Wee Tournament one year, his dazzling play earned him the nickname the White Tornado.

At age seventeen, Wayne signed his first pro contract with the Indianapolis Racers of the WHA, writing up the contract himself in longhand. Some NHL scouts who saw him play said he was too skinny, too small, too slow for pro hockey. His first contract was for four years and $875,000. It seemed like a huge amount of money at the time – and it was – but a few years later he was earning ten times as much.

Even in minor hockey, Wayne tucked the right side of his hockey jersey into his pants because the jerseys he was given were always too big for him. In pro hockey he tucked in the side of his jersey because it had become a habit. Besides, like most hockey players, he was superstitious. Here's a little known fact – he even used Velcro to make sure the jerseys stayed in place.

Number 99 Retired Forever

Dozens of NHL stars have seen their team jerseys lifted to the arena rafters – their numbers retired forever from play for their team. But only one number – Wayne Gretzky's Number 99 – has been retired by the entire league. No NHL player will ever wear it again. Prior to Gretzky's final game with the New York Rangers in 1999, NHL Commissioner Gary Bettman announced that Number 99 had become so associated with the greatness of Gretzky that no other player would be allowed to wear it again. At the 2000 All Star game in Toronto, in an on-ice ceremony, Gretzky and members of his family attended the formal retirement ceremonies.

Gretzky wasn't the first NHL player to wear Number 99. Five different players have worn it in league history.

Leo Bourgault and Joe Lamb wore double nines on their jerseys – both in 1934–35 with the Montreal Canadiens. Neither player wore it for more than a few games.

Forty-four years later, in 1979, Gretzky arrived in the NHL wearing Number 99. In 1977, during his junior hockey days at Sault Ste. Marie, Gretzky had been given the number. It was suggested he wear 99 because another junior player had already claimed Number 9 – the number Gretzky wanted.

Forward Wilf Paiement began wearing 99 after he was traded from Colorado to Toronto in December 1979.

Only a trivia expert would know the name of the fifth player to wear Number 99. Rick Dudley, when he was traded from the Buffalo Sabres to the Winnipeg Jets in 1981, asked for jersey Number 9.

Someone told him, "That number's taken. Wear 99 instead."

After a few days, the Jets played in Edmonton. When Oiler fans saw Dudley wearing "Gretzky's" number they were furious. Dudley was the target of their verbal abuse every time he stepped on the ice.

"Oh, they gave me an awful time," he recalls. "I couldn't wait to switch to another number."

CHAPTER 12

FAST FINAL FACTS

Did You Know?

- The national anthem of the home team has been played prior to NHL games since the 1946–47 season.

- Protective glass surrounding the boards of the rink first appeared in Maple Leaf Gardens in Toronto in 1948. Protective glass soon became mandatory in all NHL buildings.

- In 1979, all players performing in the NHL were required to wear helmets approved by the NHL Rules Committee. Those in the league prior to 1979 did not have to wear helmets. Craig MacTavish was the last NHL player to go bareheaded – he retired in 1997.

- Since 1950, a player must be eighteen years old to play for a team in the NHL. The youngest player in NHL history was Armand (Bep) Guidolin, who was only sixteen when he joined the Boston Bruins in November 1942.

- On November 28, 1982, rookie Ron Sutter made NHL history when he played in his first game for the Philadelphia Flyers. It marked the first time that five brothers played in the NHL.

- On October 20, 1993, Wayne Gretzky scored a goal and added two assists in a game featuring two Gretzkys. He played against his younger brother Brent, appearing in his second NHL game. Brent played in thirteen NHL games for Tampa Bay over two seasons, and scored one goal – 884 fewer than his older brother.

- When goalie John Tanner made his NHL debut with the Quebec Nordiques on March 31, 1990, he became the seventh netminder to play for the team that season.

- In 1983–84, Tom Barrasso, an eighteen-year-old goalie, jumped from his high-school hockey team in Acton-Boxboro, Massachusetts, to the Buffalo Sabres. Barrasso had a sensational season and won the Calder Trophy as Rookie of the Year, the Vezina Trophy as top goalie, and a First Team All Star berth.

- In 1986–87, his rookie season, goaltender Ron Hextall of the Philadelphia Flyers collected a record 105 minutes in penalties.

- The oldest rookie to win the Calder Trophy was Calgary's Sergei Makarov, a former Soviet star, who was thirty-one. Later, the NHL declared that rookies must not be over twenty-six years old.

- The 1966–67 Toronto Maple Leafs were the oldest team (average age thirty-one) to win the Stanley Cup. Their clinching 3–1 victory over the Montreal Canadiens on May 2, 1967, was the last game played in the era of the Original Six teams.

- Seven NHL goaltenders have scored goals in a game: Billy Smith (New York Islanders); Ron Hextall (Philadelphia Flyers), who did it twice; Chris Osgood (Detroit Red Wings); Martin Brodeur (New Jersey Devils), who also did it twice; Damian Rhodes (Ottawa Senators); Jose Theodore (Montreal Canadiens); and Eugene Nabokov (San Jose Sharks).

- The most shocking trade in NHL history took place on August 9, 1988, when Wayne Gretzky was dealt to the Los Angeles Kings – along with Marty McSorley and Mike Krushelnyski – in return for Jimmy Carson, Martin Gelinas, three first round draft picks, and $15 million. Gretzky's arrival in L.A. meant an extra 3000 season-ticket sales for the Kings.

• Wayne Gretzky, executive director of Canada's men's hockey team at the 2002 Olympics in Salt Lake City, had a Canadian one-dollar piece – a "loonie" – buried under the center-ice circle in the arena. He hoped it would bring Team Canada good luck. And it did. Both the men's and women's teams from Canada won gold medals. The loonie is now in the Hockey Hall of Fame.

Fascinating Records

Joe Malone scored 44 goals in twenty games in 1917–18, the first season of the NHL. His season average of 2.20 goals per game is still a record more than eighty seasons later.

• On February 18, 1928, goalie Alex Connell of the Ottawa Senators recorded his sixth consecutive shutout with a 1–0 win over Montreal. Connell's mark has never been surpassed. Connell recorded fifteen shutouts that season, but he was upstaged by little George Hainsworth of the Canadiens, who blanked opposing teams twenty-two times in forty-four games.

• On March 28, 1975, the pitiful Washington Capitols ended their record thirty-seven-game losing streak on the road with a 2–0 win over Oakland. The Caps finished the season 1-39-0 (wins-losses-ties) away from home.

• On February 2, 1977, Toronto Maple Leafs defenseman Ian Turnbull set a record for defensemen when he scored five goals in a game. It came in a 9–1 rout of the Detroit Red Wings. Turnbull took five shots on goal and scored on all of them.

• On December 19, 1984, Scotty Bowman became the NHL's winningest coach with career victory number 691. On June 13, 2002, he won his ninth Stanley Cup, beating Toe Blake's record of eight.

• On December 19, 1987, Ken Linseman of the Boston Bruins and Doug Gilmour of the St. Louis Blues scored goals just two seconds apart, to set an NHL record for the fastest two goals in a game. Gilmour's goal came off a center-ice face-off and was scored into an empty net.

• On March 23, 1994, Wayne Gretzky of the Los Angeles Kings scored career goal 802, to pass Gordie Howe and establish a new NHL record for most career goals. Gretzky finished his career with a record 894 goals, ninety-three more than Howe.

- On March 23, 1994, Teemu Selanne of the Winnipeg Jets shattered rookie scoring records with 76 goals and 132 points. No rookie since has come close to those marks. Neither has Selanne.

- In January 1997, defenseman Michel Petit set a record by playing for his ninth different NHL team. The following season he played for his tenth team – the Phoenix Coyotes.

- The Montreal Canadiens have won almost twice as many Stanley Cups as any other team. The Canadiens have captured a record twenty-four Cup wins. The Toronto Maple Leafs have won thirteen, and the Detroit Red Wings ten.

- Forward Doug Jarvis played eleven-plus seasons in the NHL without missing a game. On December 26, 1986, Jarvis broke Gary Unger's ironman record of 914 consecutive games. He went on to establish a new mark of 964 consecutive games.

- Montreal's Henri Richard holds the record for most Stanley Cup wins, at eleven.

- In 1992–93, the Montreal Canadiens won a record ten straight overtime games in the play-offs, en route to their twenty-fourth Stanley Cup.

- Maurice "Rocket" Richard may hold the record for the shortest coaching career in pro hockey. He coached the Quebec Nordiques of the WHA for just two games in 1972. Then he quit, stating, "Coaching is too hard on the nerves. I don't want to die behind the bench."

- The oldest player to play in the NHL was Gordie Howe of the Hartford Whalers. He was fifty-two and playing with his sons Mark and Marty when he called it quits after thirty-two seasons as a pro. He was also hockey's only playing grandfather.

- There's a battered puck in the Hockey Hall of Fame in Toronto that was used during a game between Minnesota and Los Angeles back in the 1970s – it was the only puck used for the entire game. Nobody could remember that ever happening before in the NHL. On most nights, two or three dozen pucks are used to get through a game.

ACKNOWLEDGMENTS

I am grateful to Paul Patscou and Kevin Shea for their assistance. Many thanks to Steve Nease for his illustrations. Finally, I would like to thank Kathy Lowinger and the team at Tundra Books, as well as Kat Mototsune for her copyedit.

B. M.

ABOUT THE AUTHOR

Brian McFarlane, a former All American hockey player, is known as Canada's foremost hockey historian. A media member of the Hockey Hall of Fame, he has been involved in the game as a writer and broadcaster for over 50 years. For 25 of those years he was a commentator on Hockey Night in Canada and he's also worked on hockey telecasts for CBS, NBC, and ESPN. He has written more than 50 books about the game – about the same number of books written by his father Leslie McFarlane, who was also known as Franklin W. Dixon, the original author of the Hardy Boys books. At age 70, Brian still plays the game twice a week and has six hockey-playing grandchildren.